Inviting Transformation
Presentational Speaking for a Changing World

Sonja K. Foss
Ohio State University

Karen A. Foss
University of New Mexico

WAVELAND

PRESS, INC.

Prospect Heights, Illinois

For information about this book, write or call:

    Waveland Press, Inc.
    P.O. Box 400
    Prospect Heights, Illinois 60070
    (847) 634-0081

#30389563

Acknowledgments

Our special thanks to Sally Miller Gearhart and Sonia Johnson for sharing with us their notions of transformation that are at the heart of this book. Ongoing conversations with several others about these ideas also were invaluable: Karen Carlton, Deborah Fort, Cindy L. Griffin, Josina M. Makau, and Ann Skinner-Jones. Thank you for inspiring and illuminating many of the ideas that created this book. Sonja's feminist advisees at Ohio State University also supplied valuable insights about translating theory into practice: Kimberly Barnett Gibson, Gail J. Chryslee, Deb Greene, D. Lynn O'Brien Hallstein, Cristina Lopez, Helene Shugart, and Catherine Egley Waggoner.

We tried out earlier versions of this book on students—those in Sonja's course, Presentational Speaking in the Organization, at Ohio State University in the spring of 1993; and those in Karen's course, Fundamentals of Speech Communication, at Humboldt State University in the fall of 1992. We appreciate your patience, insights, and confirmation that we were on the right track. We also wish to apologize to our students in previous public speaking classes for providing you with such a limited vision of presentational speaking.

Several others helped transform our ideas into manuscript form. Thanks to Neil Rowe and Carol Rowe for trusting us and our vision for this book. Robert Trapp and Gail J. Chryslee read an earlier version of the manuscript; we are grateful for your willingness to read quickly and to offer valuable and honest feedback. We also wish to thank Marcel Allbritton and Joseph Milan for their assistance with the instructor's manual.

We also wish to thank our mother, Hazel M. Foss, who thought we were arriving for a vacation only to have us arrive with this book to be finished instead. Thanks for putting up with our piles of papers, long hours of editing, and many trips to the copy shop.

Finally, many thanks to Anthony J. Radich and Stephen W. Littlejohn for enduring yet another book with patience, humor, and love.

Contents

Chapter One

Inviting
Transformation

Presentational speaking is an invitation to transformation. Speakers initiate communication with others because they are seeking opportunities for growth and change and because they believe they can offer such opportunities to others. As a result of communication, an audience may accept a speaker's invitation and leave the interaction changed in some way. A speaker, too, may re-think ideas and gain new insights as a result of the interaction that occurs. This notion that presentational speaking is an invitation to transformation, which is crucial to understanding and applying the principles of speaking discussed in the rest of this book, can be clarified by exploring the primary concepts it entails— presentational speaking, transformation, and invitation.

Presentational Speaking

When you think about giving a speech or making a presentation, what probably comes to mind is a situation in which one person is standing in front of an audience composed of at least several people and probably more. The speaker does the talking, and any oral participation by the audience, more often than not, is limited to asking questions at the end of the speech. You probably associate this kind of speaking with public settings such as lecture halls, classrooms, senate chambers, courts of law, churches, and campaign rallies. If you suffer from stage fright at all, this is the kind of speaking situation that tends to make you nervous.

In contrast to public speaking is conversation or interpersonal communication, where two or three people talk informally, with everyone participating equally in the interaction. This type of interaction, which most people find comfortable and enjoyable, usually is associated with private places such as homes or offices or perhaps places where private spaces can be created within public spaces, such as restaurants or bars.

Some oral communication cannot easily be put only into one format or the other; it can occur in conversational formats as well as in more formal speech contexts. We have chosen to call this kind of communication *presentational speaking*, and it is distinguished by two features. The first is that one person has more responsibility for the communication than do the others involved in the interaction. Perhaps that person has been asked by others to share her perspective on a subject, she has an idea she thinks will be useful to her co-workers, or she might be leading a discussion to generate ideas to solve a problem. For whatever reason, she has been given a greater role in the interaction, and other participants will expect more from her than they will from the others involved. Her communication will be somewhat more important than theirs in creating the nature, tenor, and environment of the interaction.

A second feature of this kind of oral communication is that at least one of the individuals involved in the interaction has done some thinking about the message or the ideas to be conveyed prior to the interaction. This person will not always have had a lot of time to prepare, but he will have in mind a goal for speaking, the basic message he wants to convey, and some thoughts about how to present that message.

Presentational speaking is the kind of oral communication with which this book is concerned. It deals with communication in which you have more responsibility for the communication than others in the interaction and in which you have had some prior preparation time. This communication may occur in the format of a public speech, a private conversation, or something in between. It simply involves some kind of presentation—even if it is only a few sentences long and is designed to get discussion started.

Presentational speaking, then, involves a variety of forms. The answers a candidate gives during a job interview constitute presentational speaking; the interviewer in this situation also is engaged in presentational speaking. A coach who gives a pep talk to a wrestling team is giving a presentation, as is a new manager who begins the first meeting with her staff by introducing herself. In all of these situations, one person has primary responsibility for communicating a message thought about ahead of time. When members of a group explore an issue together to figure out what they know and believe about it, they also are engaged in presentational speaking. Although this interaction produces presentations that may contain many of the hesitations, incomplete thoughts, and overlaps of spontaneous conversation, it counts as presentational speaking because the convener of the meeting has thought about the issue, asks others to participate, and assumes responsibility for starting the discussion.

Transformation

Transformation means growth or change. It may involve changing your opinion on an issue, gaining information about a subject you did not have before, or adopting a new behavior. Transformation also includes the more subtle kind of change that occurs when you incorporate new information into your systems of thought, allowing you to imagine and generate new ideas. A student at Ohio State University, Sherveen Lotfi, provides a good summary of this kind of transformation, which he hopes his presentations facilitate: "I'm hoping that after the speech is over, the kernels of information represented by the key words will expand in their minds as they did in mine and lead to other images. . . . I try to challenge them to take the next step on their own and to infer additional conclusions based on their own circumstances and understanding."[1]

Transformation happens only through the process of interaction; it cannot occur in isolation. When, for example, you see your position as the only right or correct one and are not willing to consider or to try to understand other positions, transformation is not possible. Neither can it occur when one perspective is privileged over others. Transformation is generated when you share your perspective with others—when it is subject to comparison with other perspectives in a process of discovery, questioning, and re-thinking. The transformation that may be engendered in presentational speaking, then, is not the result of the skill or expertise of one speaker. If it occurs, it results from the exchange and interaction to which the speaker's presentation contributes. Your role as a speaker is to keep the conversation going—to sustain interaction—so that new ways of thinking and acting are able to emerge.

Invitation

Invitation is a critical concept in the notion that presentational speaking is an invitation to transformation.[2] Any change that results from presentational speaking is not forced on the audience. Your efforts are directed at enabling transformation—making it possible for those who are interested—not imposing it on those who are not. The speaker's invitation is an offering, an opening, an availability—not an insistence. Some in the audience may choose to accept this invitation; others will not. Your communication may appear to change thinking and behavior, but you do not and cannot change others. Such changes are the results of decisions by listeners who choose to hear others or to learn from others. Transformation occurs only through the process of self-change generated by interaction with other perspectives.

When you offer an invitation to transformation and do not impose it, you recognize that audience members have had experiences and hold perspectives that are as valuable and legitimate as your own. You view audience members as the authorities on their own lives who hold the beliefs they do and act as they do for reasons that make good sense to them. You respect, then, the integrity and authority of audience members by offering your ideas to them rather than imposing your ideas on them.

Sherveen Lotfi uses a metaphor of baking cookies to convey this notion: "Giving a speech is like sharing cookies we've baked with the people around us. They may or may not like them. I hope that the cookies are so tasty that the people who ate them want to go and bake some of their own."[3] Audience members may refuse the invitation—may not take any cookies from the plate that is passed—for any number of legitimate reasons.

Although you cannot force transformation on your audience, what you can do is create, through the communicative options you select, an environment in which others may change if they are inclined to do so. As Sally Miller Gearhart explains, "No one can change an egg into a chicken. If, however, there is the potential in the egg to be a chicken . . . then there is the likelihood that in the right environment (moisture, temperature, the 'external conditions for change') the egg will hatch."[4]

Four external conditions are particularly critical for the creation of an environment in which self-change may take place—safety, value, freedom, and openness.[5] When these conditions are present, self-change is more likely to occur. As you prepare your presentation, you can select communicative options that either facilitate or impede the development of these conditions in your particular speaking situation.

Safety is the condition of feeling free from danger, of feeling secure. Your communication contributes to a feeling of safety when you let audience members know that the ideas and feelings they share with you will be received with respect and care. You also help create a safe environment when you do not hurt, degrade, or belittle your audience members or their beliefs. Providing a means for your audience members to order their world in some way so it seems coherent and makes sense to them is another way to contribute to their feeling of safety. When people feel their sense of order is threatened or challenged, they are more likely to cling to familiar ways of thinking and to be less open to possibilities for change. When you create safety in a speaking situation, audience members trust you, are not fearful of interacting with you, and feel you are working with and not against them.

Value is the acknowledgment that your audience members have intrinsic or immanent worth. You convey that you value your listeners when you allow all participants in the interaction to be heard. But valuing them means more than recognizing their right to participate in the conversation; it involves encouraging their participation—inviting them to share their perspectives with you and listening carefully when they do. When audience members' perspectives vary widely from yours, try to understand them by learning more about the individuals in your audience and trying to discover why they might have developed the perspectives they have. Making the effort to think from the standpoint of your audience members—trying to make vivid in your own mind their perspectives—also is a way of valuing them. When value is created in a speaking situation, audience members feel that you care about them, understand their ideas, and allow them to contribute in significant ways to the interaction.

Freedom, the third condition whose presence in an environment contributes to the possibility of transformation, is the power to choose or decide. You contribute to the creation of a sense of freedom when you create opportunities for others to develop and select their own options from alternatives they themselves have created. Freedom also is developed when you do not place restrictions on the interaction. Participants can bring any and all matters to the interaction for consideration; no subject matter is privileged subject matter, and all presuppositions can be challenged. If audience members do not make the choices you would like them to make, you do not ban their participation from the interaction, halt the interaction, or sever your relationship with them. They are free in the interaction to make their own choices and decisions.

If communication is to create an environment in which transformation may occur, it cannot deliberately exclude any perspectives. In fact, you want to encourage participants in the interaction to incorporate as many perspectives as possible to ensure that the greatest number of ideas is considered. The condition of openness, then, is the fourth characteristic of a potentially transformative environment. It involves genuine curiosity about and a deliberate seeking out of perspectives different from your own or from the standard view. It involves exploring carefully and thoughtfully these other perspectives and approaching the differences they represent with an attitude of appreciation and delight.

With our emphasis on presentational speaking as a means to create the conditions of safety, value, freedom, and openness and thus to invite transformation, we are privileging growth and change. We are suggesting that being open to being changed is desirable and is better than developing a rigid position or coming to a "correct" understanding of a subject and sticking to it. Our primary reason for this focus is that many of the problems facing the world today seem to be the result of people's beliefs that they hold the only right positions, which they try to impose on others. The conflicts among people in the former Yugoslavia, between the pro-choice and anti-abortion forces, and between loggers and environmentalists in the Pacific Northwest, for example, seem to be the result of such rigidity. On a more personal level, misunderstandings, conflicts, and severed relationships are often the result of an unwillingness to yield on positions and a lack of openness to those held by others. We believe understandings are more likely to develop, differences are more likely to be bridged, and creative and imaginative solutions are more likely to be generated when people are open to the possibility of transformation.

Because we have chosen to privilege the opportunity for transformation, the kind of speaking dealt with in this book may look very different from the kinds of speaking with which you are familiar. We are not interested in the kind of speaking that occurs when a speaker intimidates audience members, making them afraid to speak and humiliating them when they do; the environment that results from this type of presentation is not one in which individuals feel safe or valued. We are not interested in the kind of speaking that is designed to showcase the talents of the speaker and to enhance his status or ego; this kind of speaking devalues and is closed to the potential contributions of others involved and is not directed at encouraging an exchange of perspectives. The kind of speaking covered in this book also will not be relevant to those who engage in the kind of competitive speaking where the goal is to overpower others' positions by establishing the superiority of their own. This kind of speaking, again, does not create an environment in which others feel valued and free to hold their own perspectives. Although you may find yourself involved in speaking situations in which such communication occurs, we hope that your familiarity with and skill in using the model presented in this book will enable you to help convert those situations into ones of safety, value, freedom, and openness.

The remainder of the book deals with various ways in which you invite transformation through presentational speaking. Chapter 2 is a discussion of your interactional goals—the various reasons you might have for offering such invitations and entering interactions. Chapter 3 deals with the process of analyzing the speaking situation so that the communicative options you choose in the process of preparing your presentation will facilitate rather than impede possibilities for transformation. The process of forming your presentation is the subject of chapters 4 through 8. Chapter 4 covers the process you go through as you focus your subject and generate main ideas and a commitment statement. Chapter 5 covers the construction of connections among your main ideas. The process of elaborating on your ideas is dealt with in chapter 6, and in chapter 7, means for disclosing the form of your presentation to your audience are discussed. Chapter 8 is concerned with the last stage of the forming process—creating your speaking plan and the notes from which you will speak. Chapter 9 deals with the actual delivery of your presentation. At the end of the book are sample presentations designed to show a wide range of communicative options that issue invitations to transformation in various ways.

Chapter Two

Developing Interactional Goals

The process of presentational speaking usually is initiated when you have a perspective on a subject you want to offer to others or someone invites you to share your ideas. When you make the decision to enter a communicative situation, you have a personal reason for doing so. This is your interactional goal, the goal you hope to accomplish by initiating or joining an interaction. In the terms in which we usually think about invitations—invitations to parties or other social events—you are saying, with your interactional goal, why you decided to host this particular event. What do you hope it gives you? What do you hope to offer others with this event? You are not the only one, of course, who enters the communicative situation with an interactional goal or goals. Your audience members also have goals, and they will choose to accept your invitation—to join you in the interaction—for reasons of their own.

Five of the most common interactional goals—those that encompass the essential functions for which humans communicate—are: (1) To assert individuality; (2) To build community; (3) To articulate a perspective; (4) To secure adherence; and (5) To discover knowledge and belief. In a communicative situation, you probably will find that you are interacting for one or more of these reasons.

To Assert Individuality

All speakers continually engage in communication that reveals who they are as persons. You reveal your identity and your uniqueness, for example, through your clothing; where you live; the kinds of transportation you use; the friends you have; your major in school; and your choice of occupation. In some instances, however, the assertion of individuality is the focus of your communication, and you select this interactional goal as your way of inviting transformation. The assertion of individuality is your interactional goal when, for example, you interview for a job, introduce yourself to your employees when you are hired as their manager, introduce yourself on the first day of class to other students, or converse with someone you would like to know better.

In a presentation featuring this goal, projection of your personality and assertion of who you are as a unique individual receive primary emphasis. As you reveal something about your values, beliefs, and experiences, you highlight certain of your qualities and roles over others and help your audience members come to a better understanding of who you are. As a result, you hope they will see you as someone with whom they will want to continue to interact—perhaps because you offer fresh and insightful perspectives on the world or you have knowledge and experiences in which they are interested. Through asserting individuality, you also contribute to the development of a feeling of safety in your audience. Audience members will feel more safe and comfortable interacting with you because they will understand better the kinds of influences that guide your decisions and actions, some of which may affect them.

The invitation to transformation inherent in the interactional goal of asserting individuality, then, is one in which you share yourself and encourage others to do the same to establish an atmosphere of trust, respect, and familiarity that encourages continued interaction. This atmosphere, in turn, will enable you and your audience to work and think together, to learn from each other, and possibly to be transformed by your interaction.

To Build Community

At times, the interactional goal you choose is designed to build community. Your efforts to accomplish this goal are directed at reminding audience members of what they already know and share with one another—calling up for them familiar knowledge, themes, beliefs, values, and patterns. The stability of the community is accorded highest value in presentations prompted by this interactional goal, with the collective common good valued over the individual good. In this type of speaking, you place a high premium on the collective over the singular identity—on "we" rather than "I." There may be no sharp division between you as the speaker and the audience, with both you and your audience involved in presenting and listening. A presentation built on this goal, then, is geared toward others rather than toward your own personal enhancement or gain. In fact, a self-focus, no matter how gifted or imaginative, is damaging to you as the speaker if your goal is to build community.

Efforts to build community invite transformation by contributing to a shared sense of value and ease with one another within a community. As community members are reminded of their commonalities and share meanings and experiences, they are able to use those elements that unify them to explore diverse ideas openly in a supportive environment, to take collective action, and to manage conflict in healthy ways.

When you invite transformation through efforts to build community, your selection of communicative options is guided by the degree of harmony present in the community. To maintain harmony in a community where it already exists, your focus is on strengthening the social bond, calling the audience to a collective experience, and constructing and validating a common worldview. At other times, you must create community because harmony has been disrupted—the community order is threatened or has been destroyed. In such cases, you attempt to re-create order and shared meaning, to energize the group around common perspectives, and to neutralize obstacles to harmony.

Presentations in which the interactional goal is building community include a pep talk to members of an athletic team that has just formed or that has been demoralized by a string of losses, a staff meeting called to resolve conflicts, or the ritual communication that occurs at weddings or baby showers. Farewell addresses presented to someone leaving an organization or humorous, after-dinner speeches are other examples of presentations developed around an interactional goal of community building.

To Articulate a Perspective

Your invitation to transformation may have the interactional goal of articulating a perspective. When this is your goal, you share information about a subject and present your point of view on it in order to enhance understanding of the subject by all participants in the interaction. You provide the fullest, most complete expression of your perspective, based on thorough research into and careful thinking about why you came to hold that perspective rather than another. Articulating a perspective requires that you bring to bear on a subject all of the resources available to you in serious, reflective consideration. You encourage others involved in the interaction to do similar research and to present their perspectives so that as much information as possible is available to everyone.

The interactional goal of articulating a perspective might be used in a situation in which various individuals are meeting to facilitate the development of the arts in a community. The program administrator representing the state arts council would articulate the arts council's perspective, telling about the resources available to the community from that funding source. The director of the arts center in the area would articulate her perspective about what kinds of arts activities are needed in the community. The director of a social services agency in the community might articulate a perspective about the kinds of arts activities that would be most appealing to young people in the community. A decision about how to develop the arts then would be made on the basis of the information offered by all of these different perspectives. At other times, the perspectives presented are different opinions on a controversial issue, with each person involved in the interaction expressing a particular viewpoint. This would be the case, for example, when teachers who have different ideas of what courses should be included in a curriculum all express their different ideas at a staff meeting.

One form that the articulation of a perspective may assume, particularly in a hostile situation or when a prevailing perspective is very different from the one held by the speaker, is re-sourcement.[6] Re-sourcement involves the choice not to participate in a dominant system or not to accept as a given a particular framing of an issue; as a result, a perspective emerges that is different from and challenges that of the established system or individual. It involves two processes: (1) Disengagement or separation from the system; and (2) Creative development of an alternative way to articulate the issue. This form of communication is called *re-sourcement* because it involves drawing energy from a new source—a source other than the system that initially framed the issue.

Although a refusal to engage in a conflict often is interpreted negatively by those within an established system, it can constitute a positive response to a situation. Re-sourcement enables you to continue to value others because you do not allow them to violate your integrity as a person. Re-sourcement also opens up possibilities for a greater array of options for communication in the future— you later may be able to select interactional goals that are more likely to create an environment in which growth and change may occur. As a result of re-sourcement, you may go on to articulate your perspective in more traditional ways—within the established system—or to build community, for example. Re-sourcement may create an open space, then, in which a wider variety of communicative options are possible. Opportunities for transformation may emerge that may have seemed virtually impossible to create at the start of an interaction.

An example of re-sourcement as a means of articulating a perspective is provided by author and activist Starhawk, who describes an incident that followed the blockade of the Livermore Weapons Lab in California to protest the development of nuclear weapons there. She and other women were arrested and held in a school gym. During their confinement, a woman ran into the gym, chased by six guards. She dove into a cluster of women, and they held on to her as the guards pulled at her legs, trying to extract her from the group. The guards were on the verge of beating the women when one woman sat down and began to chant; the other women did the same. Starhawk describes the reaction of the guards: "They look bewildered. Something they are unprepared for, unprepared even to name, has arisen in our moment of common action. They do not know what to do. And so, after a moment, they withdraw. . . . In that moment in the jail, the power of domination and control met something outside its comprehension, a power rooted in another source.''[7]

Another example of the use of re-sourcement as a response to a hostile or dangerous situation that is not likely to allow all perspectives to be heard is found in the movie, *The Long Walk Home*. The movie recreates the boycott by African Americans of buses in Montgomery, Alabama; the protest was aimed at securing seats on a first-come-first-served basis regardless of race. At one point, women involved in and sympathetic to the boycott are surrounded by a group of jeering men who threaten violence. The women respond by singing a gospel song, and the men back away without harming the women.

In other instances, re-sourcement may be used to articulate a perspective that is widely variant from an unquestioned, prevailing perspective. This was the case when Adrienne Rich was awarded the National Book Award's prize for poetry in 1974. When she accepted the award, she read a statement that had been prepared by Audre Lorde, Alice Walker, and herself—all of whom had been nominated for the prize. In the statement, the three women announced that they were accepting the award together and would share the prize: ''We believe that we can enrich ourselves more in supporting and giving to each other than by competing against each other; and that poetry—if it *is* poetry—exists in a realm beyond ranking and comparison.''[8] (Their complete statement is one of the sample presentations included at the end of this book.)

In articulating a perspective, either through re-sourcement or the expression of a perspective to others as part of a system, you invite audience members to consider the perspective, think critically about it, and develop their own perspectives equally thoroughly. The interchange of multiple, carefully developed perspectives creates the potential for transformation for those involved in the interaction.

To Secure Adherence

In some instances, the invitation to transformation you offer will be the result of an interactional goal to encourage others to change in particular directions. In these cases, your efforts are directed toward securing the adherence of others to your perspective—to persuading them to think as you do, to accept your proposal, or to act in ways you believe are most appropriate. When you invite transformation through persuasion, your invitation is less an invitation than it is a request.

You may choose persuasion as your interactional goal for a number of reasons. Perhaps you perceive that your community is facing imminent danger, and you speak to urge community members to remove the source of danger or to take the steps necessary to neutralize it. Perhaps an important decision must be made quickly, so you seek to gain others' adherence to your proposed plan of action because of time constraints. You also might believe strongly in a product and its benefits to others and want your audience to choose it over others available in order to realize those benefits. Another common situation in which your interactional goal is to seek adherence is when you interview for a job—a job you really would like to have and where you believe you could make a meaningful contribution to an organization. As you do your best at the interview, you are seeking the support of the interviewer for your candidacy.

Efforts directed at securing adherence involve your intent to encourage someone to choose to change. In your invitation to transformation with this interactional goal, you have a particular change in mind for your audience and employ strategies that make change on the part of audience members desirable and likely. The process of securing adherence, then, is essentially one of conversion; your aim is not to destroy your opponents and overpower your audience members and their perspectives but to convince them that your perspective is better than theirs. With this interactional goal, you seek to engage audience members and motivate them to adopt your perspective or to act as you desire. Although you want audience members to change in a particular direction, however, they still participate fully in that change process, freely choosing if they will adhere to your claim.

To Discover Knowledge and Belief

In some interactions, the speaker and audience are unsure of what they know and believe and seek to discover and sort out together the information, experiences, and feelings they have relevant to a subject. This interactional goal is one of discovering knowledge and belief. Together, the speaker and audience members explore a subject to discover what they know about it, believe about it, and thus if and how they will choose to be transformed by it.

You might select the goal of discovering knowledge and belief when you seek to solve a problem that plagues you and your co-workers; when you lead a class discussion as a teacher; or when a friend talks to you about the difficulties he is having in an intimate relationship. When the President calls a summit to gather information about a problem and to explore possible solutions to it, the interactional goal he is using is one of discovering knowledge and belief.

With a goal of discovering knowledge and belief, one person has primary responsibility for initiating the communication, but the interaction takes place in a dyad or group, with the opportunity for participation available to everyone. Your efforts in this kind of interaction, then, are directed to interviewing or leading group discussions, where your primary responsibilities include framing the subject for discussion, guiding those present through an analysis and investigation of the subject, and summarizing the insights produced by the discussion. In this situation, you act much like a midwife, coaching and assisting others as they present their knowledge and perspectives. You do not enter the interaction with a claim or proposal you already have developed and that you want others to come to accept in the course of the discussion. Instead, you genuinely do not know what you think or believe—you hold no perspective yet or, at best, an unformed, tentative one—and allow the discussion to direct the development of your perspective.

All five of these interactional goals can be used as the basis for creating the conditions for transformation—safety, value, freedom, and openness. From all five goals, you also can create just the opposite conditions. When a teacher introduces herself to a class on the first day of school, for example, with an interactional goal of asserting individuality, she may create an atmosphere in which students feel safe and valued. She also could choose to assert individuality in such a way that she arrogantly communicates superiority, and her students feel intimidated and vulnerable. Similarly, the interactional goal of securing adherence might be used by someone who presents a proposal to co-workers that she would like them to adopt. She can present her ideas in a way that indicates an openness to and valuing of the proposals of others and a willingness to continue to interact with them even if her proposal is not adopted. The same presentation, however, can be given in a way that threatens and devalues the others present, silences their ideas, and generally stops the interaction.

This book is designed to enable you to use any of the interactional goals to create presentations that establish an atmosphere characterized by safety, value, freedom, and openness. As you will see in the chapters that follow, you have many communicative options available for enacting your interactional goals. The choices you make will determine whether or not your presentation creates a potentially transformative environment.

Analyzing the Speaking Environment

With the identification or selection of your interactional goal or goals, you are ready to begin an analysis of the components of your specific speaking environment to discover whether they facilitate or hinder possibilities for transformation. If your analysis reveals that certain factors will facilitate creation of a transformative environment, you know these are the factors to emphasize as you begin to form your ideas into a presentation. If other factors appear as obstacles to transformation, adjust them or neutralize their impact so you are able to develop, as much as possible, the conditions of safety, value, freedom, and openness in the interaction.

The four primary factors of the speaking environment to consider are the setting, audience, speaker, and subject. Below is a list of questions to stimulate your thinking about these factors and their possible impacts on the environment you are creating. These questions should be seen only as starting points; the particulars of your speaking situation will suggest other environmental factors to consider.

Setting

Date.   What is the date on which you are speaking? Is there anything unusual about it for either you or your audience?

Hour.   At what time of day are you speaking? Is it early? Late? At a time when you and your audience members are functioning at peak levels?

Meeting place.   What are the characteristics of the place in which you are speaking? Is it indoors or outdoors? What is the shape and size of the space? Are there acoustical problems? What is the temperature? What kinds of lights are available in the room? Will the audience be standing, sitting on chairs, or sitting on the floor? How are the chairs arranged? In rows? In a circle?

Size of audience.   How large is your audience? Are you speaking to one person? To a small group? To a large group? Can the space accommodate your audience comfortably?

Purpose for gathering.   What is the purpose of the event, meeting, or interaction at which your presentation will be given? To conduct business? To socialize? To solve a problem? To reinforce community ties?

Order of events.   What or who precedes and follows your presentation? Are other presentations planned? On what subjects? How long has your audience been listening to presentations before yours? Are food and refreshments to be served and, if so, when?

Time constraints.   How much time do you have for your present-ation?

If an analysis of your setting, for example, tells you that you will be speaking following dinner at a conference that has been going on all day, you can assume that your audience members probably will be tired—tired of sitting, tired of listening to speakers, and tired of thinking. Consequently, they are not likely to be particularly open to hearing from you and to allowing your communication to serve as a catalyst for change. Instead, they are likely to stick with their current ways of thinking because they are interested in other things—perhaps joining others for after-conference partying or going home to bed.

To convert this obstacle into a dimension that facilitates transformation, speak on a subject of special interest to your audience. Think about ways to involve your listeners and to secure their participation in a discussion of the subject rather than simply presenting your ideas to them. Keep your presentation short. In general, select as communicative options those that enhance the contributions the setting makes to the environment you are creating.

Audience

Age.   How old are your audience members?

Sex.   Are the members of your audience women or men?

Family status.   To what kinds of family structures do your audience members belong? Are they single? Cohabitating partners? Gay or lesbian couples? Married couples? Do they have children?

Economic status.   What is the economic standing of your audience? Lower class? Middle class? Upper class?

Educational status.   How much formal education has been completed by your audience members? Grade school? High school? Vocational school? College? In what other ways have they pursued knowledge and understanding? Workshops and seminars? Apprenticeships? Continuing education programs? Community classes? Reading?

Occupation.   If your audience members are employed, what are their occupations? Are they in service professions? In business? In technical trades? In the arts?

Place of residence.   In what region of the country do your audience members live? A rural area? A small town? A large city? Did they grow up in the region or are they transplants from elsewhere?

Religious affiliation. To what extent do your audience members embrace religion or spirituality? With what religious traditions do they identify?

Political affiliation. Do your audience members identify with traditional or other political parties? How important is party affiliation to them?

Cultural identities. What cultural identities are important to your audience members? Are primary identifications based on race? Ethnicity? Gender? Sexual orientation? Do they claim membership in cultures based on particular beliefs or interests?

Knowledge of subject. How much do your audience members know about the subject of your presentation?

Interest in subject. To what degree do your audience members care about your subject?

Perspective on subject. What are the perspectives of your audience members on your subject? If the subject is controversial, what positions do your audience members hold on it? What experiences of audience members are likely to influence the perspectives they hold?

Receptivity to change. How committed are your audience members to their perspectives? To what degree are your audience members willing to yield their perspectives?

Homogeneity. To what degree are your audience members homogeneous? Are they all, for example, the same age? The same sex? Members of the same political party?

To give you an idea of how your analysis based on audience factors might proceed, suppose you discover, in your analysis, that your audience is composed of both women and men. This fact, in itself, is neither an obstacle nor an advantage for the creation of the four conditions that make up a potentially transformative environment—safety, value, freedom, and openness. But to insure that this dimension of the audience does not become a hindrance, develop your subject using communicative options that have appeal for and refer to the experiences of both women and men. Use sex-neutral language so that you include rather than alienate the women in your audience and to suggest that you value them as much as you do the men. Avoid using terms, for example, that suggest that all your audience members and perhaps all people are male. Instead of using a term such as *mankind*, for example, use *humankind* or *people*. A term such as the generic *he*, used to refer to a person of either sex, would be replaced by *she or he*; by a plural construction using *they*; or by alternating *she* and *he*, the option used in this book. *You guys* would become *you all* or just plain *you*. Your use of sex-neutral language suggests that you value the contributions and participation of all members of your audience and thus helps establish the conditions necessary for an environment of transformation.

Speaker

Position.   What is your position, title, or rank? How is it likely to be perceived in this situation?

Attitude toward self.   How do you feel about yourself in this speaking situation? Confident? Excited? Tentative? Intimidated? Scared?

Cultural identities. Which of your cultural identities are evident? Will you choose to reveal some that are not? Race? Ethnicity? Gender? Sexual orientation? How will these identities affect the audience's perceptions of you and your presentation?

Speaking competences. What kinds of communicative competences are required in this situation? The ability to explain clearly? To lead a discussion? To generate excitement? How confident are you about your ability to demonstrate these skills? Do you experience communication anxiety that may interfere with your communicative competence?

Vulnerabilities.   Are there aspects of the speaking situation that make you feel vulnerable? Are they related to your subject? Communication ability? Relationship with your audience?

Attitude toward audience. What is the nature of your relationship with your audience? Affection? Respect? Compassion? Irritation? Frustration? Do you have prejudices that may affect your attitude toward your audience?

Previous experience with audience. Are your audience members acquainted with you? From what context? What experiences, if any, have you previously had with your audience that might affect this situation?

Knowledge of subject. How much do you know about the subject of the interaction?

Comfort with subject.   How comfortable are you talking about this subject?

Perspective on subject.   What is your initial perspective or point of view on the subject?

Receptivity to change. How committed are you to your perspective? To what degree are you willing to yield your perspective?

In your analysis of the factors that you as the speaker bring to the speaking situation, you may find that one such dimension is your lack of skill in a particular form of communication. If you feel less comfortable with particular communicative options, avoid them, if possible. If you feel removed and distanced from your audience by standing behind a podium and prefer face-to-face interaction as you communicate, walk around the room as you speak and ask your audience members to participate. Similarly, if you feel you lack the skills to lead a discussion well, you probably will not be comfortable incorporating discussion into your presentation. If your interactional goal is to discover knowledge and belief, however, you will need to be able to do this effectively. In that case, you might ask participants to bring with them to the meeting one suggestion for solving the problem or one idea on a subject, thus ensuring that everyone has done focused, prior thinking on the subject. Prepare thoroughly for the discussion, clarifying the history of and facts about the issue; carefully plan an opening statement that incorporates this information. Develop some statements or questions you can use to encourage participation. In other words, do everything you can to turn your communicative weaknesses into strengths so they do not impede your efforts to create an environment that facilitates transformation.

Subject

Comfort level.   Is the subject a comfortable and easy one for your audience members to listen to and discuss?

Complexity.   How complex is the subject?

Nature of evidence.   What sources of information or evidence about the subject are allowed or privileged? Library research? Personal experience? Testimonials from others?

Controversial nature.   How controversial is the subject? Are there likely to be opposing perspectives on it?

Interactional goal.   What is the interactional goal guiding your presentation of the subject? Will your effort to invite transformation assume the form of asserting individuality? Building community? Articulating a perspective? Securing adherence? Discovering knowledge and belief? What expectations and constraints are generated by your goal?

Your analysis of subject dimensions may suggest, for example, that the subject you will be discussing has the potential to be a highly controversial one. Such a topic may act as a barrier to the creation of a transformative environment simply because it encourages participants to dig in and seek support for their own positions. To encourage the creation of the conditions of safety, value, freedom, and openness when a subject generates controversy is difficult, but by selecting communicative options that encourage receptivity, you can move closer to creating these conditions. For example, select as your interactional goal articulating a perspective rather than securing adherence; this will allow full presentation of multiple views and convey to participants that they are being heard. Incorporate into your presentation self-disclosure about your background and the influences that led you to adopt the perspective you hold, helping other participants understand the context for your perspective. Be careful, as you lead discussion or answer questions, not to belittle or devalue any opinions.

In the ideal environment for communication, the conditions of safety, value, freedom, and openness are necessary to insure maximal opportunities for self-change by the participants. An analysis of the dimensions of the speaking environment—setting, audience, speaker, and subject—reveals which are likely to facilitate and which are likely to obstruct the creation of a transformative environment.

Chapter Four

Focusing the Presentation

F ollowing an analysis of environmental factors relevant to your speaking situation—setting, audience, speaker, and subject—you are ready to use this information to form your presentation. Forming is simply the process of inventing, planning, and developing your presentation.

Forming your presentation involves developing both your ideas and the structure for your ideas. Although these two processes of inventing ideas and organizing them may appear to be separate, they occur simultaneously. You do not invent the ideas you want to talk about and then pour them into a particular structure or form. Neither do you select a form for your ideas and then invent ideas to fit the form. Instead, you invent content and form, ideas and structure together. As an idea changes, its form changes, and as form changes, the idea itself evolves. The processes of inventing and organizing continue to interact in dialogic fashion as you form your presentation.

As you develop your presentation, you will be engaged in five processes: (1) focusing; (2) constructing connections; (3) elaborating; (4) disclosing form; and (5) making plans.[9] Each of the next five chapters will deal with one of these steps. Although these are treated separately, they are likely to overlap considerably as you form your presentation.

In the process of focusing, you formulate the major ideas of your presentation and create a main idea that unites and integrates them. As a result of the focusing process, you will have made two major decisions about your presentation that will guide you during the remainder of the forming process. You will have formulated a commitment statement and the major ideas of your presentation.

The first decision you make in the course of the focusing step concerns your commitment statement. This is a statement you develop that indicates your initial commitment to a particular perspective in the interaction. In terms of a typical social invitation, the commitment statement is the equivalent of a commitment by the host to have done some initial thinking, planning, and preparation for the gathering—cleaning the house or apartment, decorating, and preparing refreshments. Your commitment statement communicates to the audience that you have done some initial thinking about the subject and some preparation concerning how to present the results of that initial thinking.

The commitment statement summarizes the main idea of your presentation and makes an assertion about it. Another way to think of it is as a nutshell or a gist. A commitment statement makes explicit to you what you are doing in the presentation; it guides you in developing your major ideas, omitting irrelevant information, and organizing the ideas you generate. A commitment statement is not the same as a subject or topic. A subject simply names a field, a body of knowledge, or a situation. A commitment statement communicates an assertion about a subject you intend to explore, explain, or support. A subject might be, for example, "accounting," but a commitment statement on the subject would be something like, "Accounting is a field that currently offers excellent employment opportunities."

The form your commitment statement assumes depends on your interactional goal. The various interactional goals require different kinds of commitments from speakers and thus different kinds of commitment statements. If your interactional goal is to secure adherence, for example, the commitment required of you as a speaker is that you formulate, believe, and try to support a clearly defined position on a subject. A commitment statement that involves securing adherence might be: "This organization would benefit from my proposed plan for a public relations campaign." With an interactional goal of articulating a perspective, your commitment statement might be: "I believe college students benefit from studying a foreign language." A commitment statement that accompanies an interactional goal of asserting individuality would look different still: "I want to show that I am both a competent professional and a warm, open person." If your interactional goal is to build community, your commitment statement might be something like this: "By working together, we can cope effectively with our poor working conditions." In a situation where you hope to discover knowledge and belief, a commitment statement might be: "We need to discover what we think about the voucher system for education and develop a policy on it for our school district."

The commitment statement represents only an initial commitment to a perspective; it is not a statement to which you must adhere throughout the interaction. It simply represents your preliminary thinking and perspective on a subject—and it very well may change as a result of your ongoing thinking and interaction with your audience. Implicit in the commitment statement is the recognition that the interaction is not complete without the input of the audience, and the audience has a central role to play in the further development of the commitment statement. Just as a host's vision of a party changes as the guests arrive and begin to interact, so, too, may your commitment change as a result of interaction with your audience.

Both your interactional goal and your commitment statement serve as guides for you as you develop the main ideas of your presentation. The main ideas you choose to discuss should be ones that clearly relate to and develop your commitment statement and that are congruent with the interactional goal you have in mind. These may be generated in various ways—from your own experience with and knowledge of a subject, from interviews with others, or from library research, for example.

Let's say you are going to encourage your state legislators to increase funds for alcohol-education programs for teenagers. Your interactional goal is to secure the adherence of the legislators to support your call for an increase in this segment of the budget, and your commitment statement is, "The budget for alcohol-education programs directed at under-age drinkers should be increased." You now are well on your way to identifying at least some of the major ideas you believe will be most useful to you in developing the presentation. The major ideas your statement generates initially might be: alcohol consumption is related to an increase in traffic fatalities, few teenagers in the state receive sufficient information about the negative effects of alcohol consumption, and the incidence of alcoholism among teenagers is increasing dramatically. You may not use all of these ideas in your presentation, but at this point, you want to generate as many ideas as you can relevant to your commitment statement.

The processes involved in focusing are those that get you started—clarifying where your initial commitments lie and pointing you in particular directions for the development of ideas. Formulation of your commitment statement and major ideas leads to a consideration of connections among major ideas, the next step in the forming process.

Chapter Five

Constructing
Connections

onstructing connections is the process by which you formulate
relationships among the major ideas of your presentation. At
this stage, you decide how you will connect the ideas you began
to generate in the focusing step. The forms that result are organizational patterns; they are the basic structures in which you issue
your invitation to transformation. There are no correct or right
organizational patterns that will emerge from your attention to the
relationships among your ideas. Let your own style—your personal,
unique, characteristic way of constructing connections—guide you.
You also will want to take into account any expectations generated
by environmental factors for the form of your presentation. The
subject you are discussing, your interactional goal, the genre of your
presentation (a commencement address or a presentation at a staff
meeting, for example), and the characteristics of your audience
affect the choices you make in constructing relationships among
your ideas.

Constructing relationships may be done in a variety of ways.
Two common ways are playing cards and clustering. Playing cards
is a technique in which you "play cards" with ideas or pieces of
information. You put each idea you have generated or collected on
a separate card or slip of paper and lay them out in various possible
arrangements until a pattern appears that seems to you to
encompass the information in a useful way. Cards that contain
information or data that do not fit the emerging schema are
discarded.

In clustering, a second approach to connecting your ideas, you
start with key concepts and cluster related concepts, images, and
ideas around them. Some of the clustered concepts become the
centers of new clusters and begin to generate ideas for concepts and
images associated with them. At some point in this process, you
become aware of an emerging form or organizational pattern that
connects your ideas.

Sometimes, you may find that you could use a little help in
figuring out how to organize ideas for your presentation. In this case,
you might want to turn to fixed forms of arrangement or organizational patterns as sources of possible ideas. These are common or
conventional formats that others have considered to be useful ways
of connecting ideas and, in fact, you may discover that you naturally
tend to use some of them. They should not be regarded as ideal
patterns into which you should make your ideas fit, however. These
patterns simply may provide you with leads to follow in developing
relationships among your ideas. Among these conventional organizational patterns are:

Alphabet.   The alphabet can be used as an organizational pattern for a presentation. It involves arranging ideas in alphabetical order; this is the form used to organize this list of organizational patterns. A variation of this pattern is the structuring of a presentation around an acronym such as SAFE to discuss earthquake preparedness. *S* might stand for securing the environment, *A* for advance planning, *F* for family meeting place, and *E* for emergency supplies.

Category.   A category format is suggested by a set of categories that either is relatively standard for your subject or naturally arises from it. The major components, types, questions, functions, or qualities of a subject can be used as its organizational schema. The subject of leadership, for example, readily breaks down into the categories of different models of leadership or the categories of qualities of a good leader; either one could be used to organize your ideas.

Causal.   A causal organizational pattern is structured around a series of causes or contributing causes that account for some effect. This pattern can be organized either by discussing how certain causal factors will produce a particular effect or by suggesting that a particular set of conditions appears to have been produced by certain causes. In a presentation on the condition of the American educational system, for example, educational consultant David Boaz spent the first part of his presentation establishing that schools do not work (the effect) and the second part establishing that there is no competition and thus no incentive to improve the school system (the cause).[10]

Circle.   In a circle organizational pattern, ideas are structured in a circular progression. One idea is developed, which leads to another, which leads to another, which leads to another, which then leads back to the original idea. You might suggest to your co-workers, for example, that greater cooperation is needed among staff members. To achieve this, you propose that the group come up with some goals for working together, such as being honest with each other. Honesty may contribute to a greater feeling of trust which, in turn, may contribute to an environment in which staff members are more likely to cooperate.

Continuum.   A continuum organizational pattern is structured by gradation; objects or ideas are linked by some common quality but differ in grade, level, or degree. Using this pattern, you move from one end of the continuum to the other. You might organize a presentation using a continuum pattern by discussing ideas in the order of, for example, small to large, familiar to unfamiliar, simple to complex, or least expensive to most expensive. For a presentation

on absenteeism in a company, you might talk first about the
department with the highest rate of absenteeism and end with a
discussion of the one with the lowest rate to discover what can be
learned about the factors that contribute to absenteeism.

Elimination.   An organizational pattern of elimination begins
with a discussion of a problem, followed by a discussion of several
possible solutions to the problem. The solutions are examined in
turn and eliminated until the one preferred remains. In a
presentation on the state's budget deficit, for example, you might
suggest solutions such as imposing an additional tax on cigarettes,
implementing a sales tax, cutting state programs, and raising
property taxes. You dismiss the first three solutions for various
reasons and devote your presentation to advocating an increase in
property taxes.

Location.   Ideas are assembled in terms of spatial or geographic
relationship in an organizational pattern of location. In a
presentation on the closing of military bases in the United States,
for example, a speaker could discuss the bases to be closed in
geographical order, beginning with the Northeastern part of the
United States and moving to the Southeast, the Midwest, the
Southwest, and the Northwest.

Metaphor.   Metaphor, a comparison between two items, ideas, or
experiences, can be used as an organizational pattern that
structures a presentation. One example of this use of metaphor is
a presentation by Richard R. Kelley, the CEO of Outrigger Hotels
Hawaii. He used the metaphor of a cold to organize his ideas on how
the company could survive in recessionary times in a presentation
entitled, "Prospering in '92: How to Avoid a Cold When the World
is Sneezing."[11]

Motivated sequence.   The motivated sequence is a five-step
organizational pattern designed to encourage an audience to move
from consideration of a problem to adoption of a possible solution:

1. Attention: The introduction of the presentation is designed to
   capture the attention of audience members. In a presentation
   to high-school students on the sexual transmission of AIDS,
   for example, a speaker might begin by citing statistics on the
   number of high-school students who have AIDS and who have
   died of the disease in the United States.

2. Need: In the need step, a problem is described so that the
   speaker and audience share an understanding of the problem.
   At this point, the speaker describes the transmission of AIDS
   through sexual intercourse and suggests there is a need for
   young people to engage in honest, explicit discussion about sex
   and sexual practices with their partners.

3. Satisfaction: A plan is presented to satisfy the need created. The speaker might suggest various ways young people might initiate talk about sex with their partners.

4. Visualization: In visualization, the conditions that will prevail once the plan is implemented are described, encouraging the audience to visualize the results of the proposed plan. The reduced risk of AIDS and more open communication in relationships would be results the speaker could encourage the audience to visualize.

5. Action: The audience is asked to take action or grant approval to the proposed plan—in this case, to use the techniques offered to discuss sex more explicitly and openly with their partners.[12]

Multiple perspectives. An organizational pattern created around multiple perspectives is one in which an idea is developed or a problem or object is analyzed from several different viewpoints. In a presentation at a PTA meeting on how to deal with the drug problem in the schools, for example, you might examine the problem from several different perspectives—medical, social, legal, and educational—in order to understand it fully and to generate creative and workable solutions to it.

Narrative. In a narrative organizational pattern, ideas are structured in story form, using characters, settings, and plots. Communication professor Sally Miller Gearhart's presentation, "Whose Woods These Are," for example, consisted solely of a story that vividly conveyed her ideas about the violence implicit in many forms of communication.[13] (This is one of the sample presentations included at the end of this book.)

Narrative progression.   The organizational pattern of narrative progression consists of the telling of several stories, one after another, with the speaker following the leads or implications of one story into the next. Photographer Anne Noggle's commencement speech to the Portland School of Art provides an example of narrative progression as an organizational pattern; the presentation consisted of one story after another about her life, loosely connected by the notion that life is a feast.[14]

Perspective by incongruity.   Qualities or ideas that usually are seen as opposites or as belonging to different contexts are juxtaposed to create an organizational pattern of perspective by incongruity.[15] This form works particularly well in presentations in which discovery of knowledge is the focus because juxtaposing opposing concepts often generates new perspectives. Feminist theorist Ti-Grace Atkinson, for example, used an organizational pattern of perspective by incongruity in a presentation at Catholic

University when she juxtaposed religion and law and judged the Catholic church guilty of a number of crimes.[16]

Problem/no solution.   In the organizational pattern of problem/no solution, a problem is developed and its significance is established, but no solution to the problem is suggested by the speaker. A solution is seen as desirable and actually is anticipated, but it either comes as individual audience members draw their own conclusions or through group discussion by those present. Using this organizational pattern, a supervisor might discuss, with the staff, the morale problem in the office and then ask everyone to join in coming up with solutions to it.

Problem/solution.   A problem/solution organizational pattern begins with a discussion of a problem and concludes with a suggested solution or solutions. In a presentation to the Central States Communication Association, for example, communication professor Samuel L. Becker began by establishing as a problem the "loss of our ability—and even apparently of our desire—to work out our disagreements in a thoughtful way, in a way that seeks understanding, a way that brings others in rather than locking them out, a way that *builds* community instead of destroying it." He then went on to propose that teachers of communication take more responsibility for developing the kinds of discourse needed to deal effectively with social problems.[17]

Rogerian.   This organizational pattern, derived from the work of therapist Carl Rogers, is based on the belief that if people feel they are understood—that their positions are honestly recognized and respected—they will cease to feel threatened. Once threat is removed, listening is no longer an act of self-defense, and people are more likely to consider other perspectives. This pattern begins with a demonstration of understanding of audience members' positions. This means you must discover what your listeners' positions are—either prior to or at the beginning of the presentation—and demonstrate that you really understand and respect them. In the second part of the presentation, your own ideas are presented, taking into account what you have learned from the audience.

Space between things.   The essence of this organizational pattern is consideration of the opposite or the reverse of what usually is accorded attention or viewed as important. This pattern is particularly useful for generating new vantage points for viewing and understanding a subject. In this approach, you attend to whatever is not typically considered—the time between notes of music or the space between buildings, for example. You might focus, in a presentation on communication between the sexes, on what happens in the spaces between talk—in those silences when neither person is speaking.

Stream of consciousness. Stream of consciousness is an unfocused organizational pattern that does not contain easily identifiable connections among main ideas. It is held together by a central idea, but this idea is not as explicitly stated as it is in other organizational patterns. Careful examination of the presentation, however, usually reveals the system or idea that unites the seemingly irrelevant fragments. Garrison Keillor's monologues on his radio program, "A Prairie Home Companion," are examples of a stream-of-consciousness organizational pattern. In one monologue, for example, he discussed the sights he would show visitors to Lake Wobegon, Flag Day, a Flag Day celebration in 1958 in which the town created a living flag, gardens, porches, air conditioning, a ritual of greeting people from porches, and the Lundberg family and their sleepwalking habits—in that order.[18] (This monologue is one of the sample presentations included at the end of this book.)

Time. When the ideas of a presentation are organized according to their temporal relationships, an organizational pattern of time is used. Ideas presented in this form usually are organized chronologically—from past to present or from present to past. In discussing the economic relationship between Japan and the United States, for example, a speaker could show the chronological progression of the relationship and how it has changed over time.

Web. A web organizational pattern revolves around a central or core idea, with other ideas branching out from the core; each branching idea is a reflection and elaboration of the core. In the web form, you begin with the central idea and then explore each idea in turn, returning to the core idea and going out from it until they all have been covered. Judaic studies professor Jacob Neusner's commencement speech at Brown University in 1981 provides an example of this organizational pattern. His core idea was that higher education had failed to prepare students for the outside world. The major ideas he discussed were the faculty's lack of pride in the students' achievements, the high grades earned by students for poor performances, the forgiving world created by the professors for the students, and professors' disdain for students. Before Neusner developed each new idea, he reiterated briefly his core idea.[19]

In the connection step of the forming process, you construct the relationships among your major ideas, resulting in an organizational pattern in which the ideas you are generating are presented. Your next task is to elaborate on those ideas.

Chapter Six

Elaborating Ideas

E laborating is the process of expanding, extending, and developing the ideas that are emerging in the forming process. In the
process of elaboration, you are refining ideas into more specific
forms. An almost infinite number of forms of elaboration are
available, and the particular combination you select for a
presentation depends on your preferences and the nature of the
audience, setting, and subject.

As is the case with all of the communicative options available
to you in the forming process, some forms of elaboration for your
ideas facilitate the potential for transformation more than others.
One speaker might be uncomfortable sharing highly personal
information with a particular audience; she probably would not
choose to use personal narrative in a presentation because her own
discomfort may close off possibilities for transformation. Similarly,
an audience not used to discourse with a strong pattern of rhythm
and rhyme might be baffled or even irritated by it—again, selection
of these forms of elaboration may hinder the possibility of
transformation. Some forms of elaboration also work better with
certain interactional goals than others. If you are attempting to build
community, for instance, you will not want to use forms of
elaboration that are highly individualistic but rather those that
encourage audience members to come together.

What follows is a list of ways in which you can elaborate on
your ideas, but it is by no means comprehensive. The forms offered
in the list are designed to serve only as starting points for thinking
about how to develop your ideas into more specific information for
your audience.

Audience participation.   Audience participation is an invitation
to the audience to respond during the course of the presentation.
This form of elaboration allows you to use the ideas, comments,
or responses of the audience to develop your ideas. Audience
participation may assume a variety of forms:

1. Call/response.   Call/response is a pattern of spontaneous vocal
   and nonverbal responses from listeners in reply to a speaker's
   statements or questions that testify to the impact of the
   message. Call/response functions much as applause does; it is
   a form of affirmation and support. It tells you when the
   audience is with you and when you can move to a discussion
   of your next idea. Within this form, all audience responses are
   correct; the only incorrect response is not to respond at all.
   Civil-rights leader Jesse Jackson created a call/response
   sequence in his speech to the Democratic convention in 1988;

the audience chanted "common ground" with Jackson at regular intervals in this sequence:

> Think of Jerusalem—the intersection where many trails met. A small village that became the birthplace for the three great religions—Judaism, Christianity and Islam.
>
> Why was this village so blessed? Because it provided a crossroads where different people met, different cultures, and different civilizations could meet and find common ground.
>
> When people come together, flowers always flourish and the air is rich with the aroma of a new spring.
>
> Take New York, the dynamic metropolis. What makes New York so special?
>
> It is the invitation of the Statue of Liberty—give me your tired, your poor, your huddled masses who yearn to breathe free. Not restricted to English only.
>
> Many people, many cultures, many languages—with one thing in common, the yearn to breathe free.
>
> Common ground![20]

2. Encouragement. In encouragement, the audience simply offers encouraging remarks to a speaker without the speaker's initiation of the call/response pattern. Participants at a campaign rally, for example, might call out, "I hear you," to signal their agreement with the candidate. They might urge a speaker to continue in a particular direction by shouting, "take your time" or "speak on it." Nonverbally, audience members might offer encouragement by waving their hands in the air, whistling, giving five, jumping up and down, and clapping their hands.

3. Testimonial.   Asking the audience to offer examples from their own lives to support an idea is a testimonial, another form of audience response that may serve as elaboration of your ideas. The stories told by participants in meetings of Alcoholics Anonymous or other support groups, for example, constitute testimonials.

Audio-visual aids. Audio-visual aids are materials that supplement spoken words and thus elaborate ideas in more comprehensive ways. Such materials usually are visual—charts, graphs, photographs, and sketches—presented via media such as slides, videotapes, overhead projectors, and blackboards. But they also may enhance discourse through smell, taste, or sound, as when a speaker plays a tape recording, for example.

Comparison and contrast. In comparison and contrast, an audience comes to know about something unfamiliar through the lens of a concept or experience that is familiar. In other words, the audience comes to understand something in terms of something else. Comparison is the process of showing the similarities between the familiar and the unfamiliar; contrast, on the other hand, links items to show their differences. Activist Suzanne Pharr provided an example of contrast when she pointed out differences between the New Christian Right and the civil rights movement, in which she has been involved:

> Our work is more difficult than that of the Christian Right. Their vision is modeled on the past, the time of the television Cleavers, when the power to exclude gave a few white people security. Our vision, on the other hand, has no model because we look to our present diversity and to the future which requires building a democratic society that includes everyone.[21]

Definition. A definition tells the meaning of a word or concept in terms the audience will understand. Lawyer Patricia Roberts Harris used a definition of *law*, for example, to develop her perspective on the relationship between law and morality: "By law, I mean that body of rules and regulations established by official governmental units to control public and private behavior, the observance of which is secured by the threat of the imposition of penalties in the nature of fine, imprisonment, or withdrawal of a government granted benefit."[22] Various means of definition are available:

1. Authority.   Definition by authority is a definition offered by an expert on a subject. L. Douglas Wilder used definition by authority when he quoted Cicero in his inaugural address following his swearing in as Virginia's governor:

   > Cicero, in a parting observation, noted that "A commonwealth is not any collection of human beings . . . but an assembly of people joined in agreement on justice and partnership for the common good, and a community where civility must reign and all must live peacefully together." And we know what happened to Cicero's Rome, which could not pass on the heritage of its past to the people of its future. But we have done so; we can do so.[23]

2. Display.   In definition by display, a word or idea is explained by pointing to something visible, as a lawyer might do when showing a jury the position of stab wounds in the clothing of a crime victim to help define the act of self-defense.

3. Etymological.   An etymological definition explains the origin or derivation of a word. In a presentation supporting a boycott of a country whose policies violate the Geneva Convention, a speaker might begin by referring to the original meaning of

> *boycott.* The term developed following an incident in Ireland in 1880 in which a land agent named Captain Boycott was ostracized for refusing to reduce rents.

4. Operational. An operational definition explains how something works. A dietician talking to a group of hospital patients might define a low-fat diet operationally by saying it is one in which the average adult consumes fewer than 25 grams of fat per day.

Discussion.   Discussion is the consideration of a question through informal exploration by at least two individuals. This is a form of elaboration you may use with any interactional goal, but it is a necessary form with the goal of discovering knowledge and belief. In such speaking situations, your responsibilities as you initiate and manage the discussion include framing the subject for discussion, keeping the discussion going, and summarizing the discussion at its close.

Dreams and visions.   Dreams and visions are considered by many audiences to be powerful sources from which to learn about and understand experience. In some cultures, dreams are considered qualitatively more vital than waking experiences because they provide the opportunity to communicate with non-human forms and thus to experience alternative levels of reality. Even individuals unfamiliar with such a perspective on dreams can appreciate the fact that dreams—whether those that occur during sleep, in daydreaming, or as conscious efforts to envision a different future—can shape our experiences in significant ways. Martin Luther King, Jr.'s famous speech, "I Have a Dream," used a personal dream of the future as a primary form of elaboration.[24]

Similarly, visions—whether the inspirations and intuitions of artists or scientists, the vision quests of Native Americans, or those that occur within conventional religious contexts—are valuable sources of power, energy, and insight that may be used to elaborate ideas. Visions often are considered to involve the transfer of sacred power to human beings, and the people, animals, or natural forces such as thunder that appear in visions are seen as vehicles through which special powers or insights are passed on to them. Native American activist Walt Bresette used a vision in the form of a prophecy in a presentation at a Green Party convention to develop the idea that Native Americans coming together to reclaim their rights was timely and expected. He quoted a participant at a successful Native American protest who saw the action as the fulfillment of a vision: "'My god, it's a fulfillment of a prophecy!' he said." Bresette continued: "Oshkiibimaadizig is the term he used: a new people, he said, came together."[25]

Emotions. Although the emphasis on logic in contemporary Western culture often discourages speakers from considering emotions as a possible form of elaboration, they can be a powerful way to develop ideas. As human beings, we respond emotionally—with our feelings—as well as logically—with our minds—to what happens in our lives. Emotions are aroused indirectly through means such as narration, vivid descriptions, and display of the emotions. Mountain climber Gwen Moffat generates fear as she elaborates on the circumstances that led her to experience this emotion:

> Once I was climbing with my partner on the summit of an ice and rock ridge 10,000 feet up. Suddenly I heard a sound like singing. It was the metal head of my ice axe humming with electricity. My hair began to rise and I realized we were in the middle of the storm. It became absolutely still and we were surrounded by black clouds. In the next moment we heard a series of strikes of simultaneous thunder and lightning like one enormous explosion, which lasted several hours. There was absolutely nothing we could do, except either stand there and literally wait to be struck or keep on moving. We went on moving.[26]

Exaggeration. Overstating a point can serve to elaborate on an idea. In a commencement address at Drew University, actor Alan Alda used exaggeration as one way to develop his idea that contemporary leaders are unprincipled and unethical: "All across the country this month, commencement speakers are saying to graduating classes, we look to you for tomorrow's leaders. That's because today's leaders are all in jail."[27]

Example. The example is a short illustration, usually no longer than a sentence or two. It is a specific illustration of a category of people, places, objects, actions, experiences, or conditions that shows the nature or character of that category. Secretary of Defense Les Aspin, in a presentation delivered to the Center for Strategic and International Studies, used a series of examples of the military's performance in Operation Desert Storm to show the capability of the U.S. military:

> Six weeks of bombing with 2,000 sorties or more a day produced few casualties on our side, but it reduced the Iraqi military to a fraction of its strength. The ground phase of the war involved hundreds of thousands of U. S. troops along with those of other nations. It lasted only 100 hours. It went off brilliantly. Again, with few losses. . . . There was a lightning armored sweep to the west—the famous left hook—to get behind the enemy forces, disorient them and defeat them. It worked. It all worked.[28]

Explanation.   An explanation is a description of a term, concept, process, or proposal to make it clear and understandable. Explanations may describe what something is, as when an advisor explains to new students the requirements for a biology major. Other explanations tell how something came to be or how something works, as when a general explains to the news media and the American public how a scud missile works. Explanations also may explain why and account for the existence of a condition or present state, as when the director of an agency explains the rationale for a decision.

Facts.   Facts are statements that generally are agreed upon as true by a culture. They are pieces of information that are verifiable by direct observation, by reference to scientific findings, or because they are offered by individuals who are granted expert status on an issue. To state that the sexual transmission of AIDS is substantially decreased when condoms are used is a fact derived from scientific findings.

Figures of speech.   Figures of speech are unusual turns of language that can elaborate on ideas in particularly vivid ways. Some frequently used figures of speech include:

1. Alliteration.   Initial or middle consonants are repeated in two or more adjacent words in alliteration. A former vice president of the United States, Spiro T. Agnew, provided an example of alliteration in a speech on television news coverage when he asserted, "Normality has become the nemesis of the network news."[29]

2. Antithesis.   Antithesis involves the juxtaposition of opposing concepts or the contrast or opposition of ideas. John Kennedy's admonition in his inaugural address, "Ask not what your country can do for you, but what you can do for your country," demonstrated antithesis.[30]

3. Metaphor.   A metaphor is a comparison in which something is spoken of as something else. Metaphor is a form of comparison and contrast; you also encountered it earlier as an organizational pattern. Linda Hollies used a metaphor to describe her childhood experience with incest:

   > There has been a gigantic mountain in my life since the age of twelve or thirteen. This mountain could not be moved, and it was too overwhelming for me, a child, to attempt to climb. I didn't have the faintest idea that a mountain could be chipped away at, or even tunneled through. . . . My father brought this mountain into my world, for, you see, I am the victim of incest.[31]

4. Oxymoron.   An oxymoron is a form of antithesis or perspective by incongruity in which opposite words are placed back to back or words that normally do not belong together are paired. B. B. King's Blues Club in Memphis makes use of the oxymoron, "famous unknowns," as a label for the musicians that appear in the club. Walt Bresette used an oxymoron to close his speech to Green Party members, suggesting that to secure their rights, Native Americans must engage in "non-violent ass kickin'." [32]

5. Personification.   In personification, the speaker attributes human qualities to non-human objects or concepts. In a presentation at the Black Hills International Survival Gathering in 1980, Russell Means personified the concept of *European tradition*, giving it the human quality of capacity to conspire: "All European tradition, Marxism included, has conspired to defy the natural order of all things."[33]

6. Simile.   A simile involves a comparison, but the comparison is not as direct and therefore not as strong as it is in a metaphor. In a simile, the comparison is introduced by either *like* or *as*. In a speech presented at an arts conference, writer Andrei Codrescu used a simile to compare the arts to the effort to dam a river: "True art is, and has always been, an argument for freedom. Trying to restrict its liberty is like damming the Mississippi River. Sooner or later Old Man River gets what it wants by the sheer force of its desire."[34]

Humor.   Humor can function not just to entertain and amuse but also to elaborate on ideas. It may release listeners from preoccupation with thoughts not relevant to a presentation and may prepare them to be open to a perspective by suddenly turning their attention to a new way of thinking. Humor is appropriate as a form of elaboration only when it is relevant to the idea you are developing, as in this example, where Harvey Milk, the first openly gay super-visor elected to San Francisco's Board of Supervisors, celebrated the increasing numbers of gays and lesbians in elected office:

> About six months ago, Anita Bryant . . . said that the drought in California was because of the gay people. On November 9, the day after I got elected, it started to rain. On the day I got sworn in, we walked to City Hall and it was kinda nice, and as soon as I said the word "I do," it started to rain again. It's been raining since then and the people of San Francisco figure the only way to stop it is to do a recall petition.[35]

Myth.   Myths are traditional stories—either real or fictitious—that explain phenomena or customs and their origins. They thus express fundamental social, cultural, and religious values important to a community. In testimony before the Supreme Court in 1915, Chief Weninock of the Yakimas told the story of the origins of Native Americans as a way of elaborating on the idea that Native Americans had legitimate claims to their traditional fishing places:

> God created the Indian country and it was like he spread out a big blanket. He put the Indians on it. They were created here in this Country, truly honest, and that was the time the river started to run. Then God created fish in this river and put deer in the mountains and made laws through which has come the increase of fish and game. Then the Creator gave us Indians Life; we walked, and as soon as we saw the game and fish we knew they were made for us.[36]

Narrative. Narration as elaboration involves telling a story, usually complete with characters, settings, plots, and dialogue. You may use stories told by others or personal narratives, where you tell about your own experiences. This is the kind of narrative Patti P. Gillespie told in a presentation she gave while president of the Speech Communication Association:

> As some of you know, I try to spend part of every other summer camping in Kenya. During my last trip in Amboseli, I was awakened just before daybreak by the sound of furiously pounding hooves that grew closer and closer to my tent. There was a horrible cry that intermingled with growls until both seemed within a few feet of where I was lying. Suddenly the cries and growls stopped, and all I heard was a very deep vibrating sound. . . .
>
> Gradually, as I thought about it, the sequence became clear to me. A zebra had been fleeing a lion, who had caught it just outside my tent and was now feasting on it. The five of us in the camp would remain hostage inside our tents until the heat of the day when the lion, satisfied and sleepy, would move away from us. Very well, I thought, I will try to calm down and wait. I waited. I had only begun to regret my last night's beer when I heard what sounded like human footsteps—yes, they were human because I next heard the unmistakable sound of pots and pans. The cook was out of his tent. Thinking him slightly mad, I dressed hastily, looked out carefully, and then joined him hurriedly at the fire. "Where was the lion kill?" I asked in butchered swahili. "No lion," he said, "hyena fight."

She continues the story, eventually making the point that just as with the hyena fight, things in higher education may not be as they seem.[37]

Poetry. Poetry is the use of meaning, sound, and rhythm in language, chosen and arranged to create a concentrated imaginative awareness of and response to an experience. Ursula K. Le Guin incorporates poetry into a commencement address she gave at Bryn Mawr to encourage her listeners to speak their minds:

> Here is a disobedient woman speaking, Wendy Rose of the Hopi and Miwok people, saying in a poem called "The Parts of a Poet,"
>
>> parts of me are pinned
>> to earth, parts of me
>> undermine song, parts
>> of me spread on the water,
>> parts of me form a rainbow
>> bridge, parts of me follow
>> the sandfish, parts of me
>> are a woman who judges.[38]

Prayer.   Prayers are entreaties, supplications, or requests, usually directed at a force the audience acknowledges as a supreme being. The speaker who prays for wisdom for those about to make an important decision, for example, is using prayer as a form of elaboration.

Proverb.   Proverbs are succinct cultural sayings that express obvious truths and readily encapsulate audience members' experiences. In a sermon, Barbara Brown Zikmund cited a Yoruba proverb to elaborate on her idea that each person is an important part of God's creation: "There is an old Yoruba proverb told among the indigenous tribes of Nigeria in West Africa that expresses the same message: 'The hand of a child cannot reach the ledge; the hand of the elder cannot enter the gourd: both the young and the old have what each can do for the other.'"[39]

Pun.   Puns are plays on words based either on different words that sound alike or on various meanings of the same word. In a presentation about her work, visual artist Janet Hughes used puns to describe what her selection for inclusion in an art exhibition meant to her. One portion of her presentation included puns on the word *read*:

> She was well read.
> She became widely read.
> She painted the town
>> the picture
>> and her lips.
> Her lips were read.
> Her lips were red.[40]

(Her complete statement is one of the sample presentations included at the end of this book.)

Question.   A question or series of questions can be used to elaborate on an idea and to encourage listeners to think about the idea and to draw their own conclusions about it. Journalist Ted Koppel's commencement speech at Duke University included several questions designed to develop his idea that television packages people and ideas. He labeled this phenomenon the "Vanna factor," referring to Vanna White, the woman who turns the letters on "Wheel of Fortune." His first question followed an idea he wanted to develop: "We have no idea what, or even if, Vanna thinks. Is she a feminist, or every male chauvinist's dream?" Later in the presentation, he asked a question and gave his answer: "What then should we, or must we conclude? Whatever your merchandise, if you want to move it in bulk, you flog it on TV."[41]

Repetition and restatement.   In repetition, words or phrases are repeated exactly; in restatement, an idea is repeated using different words. Both forms of elaboration result in a sense of building or piling and thus serve to reinforce an idea. A Yoruba masquerade chant uses repetition to convey the idea of the supreme power of death:

> On the day death would kill the rich man
> Money would be of no avail
> On the day death would kill the medicine man
> The charm that locks up man's intentions,
> The one that stupefies one
> The one that makes one look like a fool
> The one that arrests one's movements,
> Indeed, everything will perish.
> On the day death will kill the great priest,
> Gentle winds will carry off all his papers.[42]

Ritual.   Rituals are set forms or systems of rites in which members of a community participate. Often handed down from generation to generation, rituals and ceremonies function to connect community members to their heritage, community, or universe and, through that connection, to generate feelings of power and wholeness. Author Diane Stein often engages participants in her workshops in rituals designed to create changes in consciousness. In her "Croning" ritual, for example, a woman who is undergoing a transition—menopause, retirement, or her last child's departure from home—is given tangible or verbal gifts by each of those present.[43] In the African-American community, men sometimes engage in communication rituals that demonstrate allegiance to the group and communicate an identity—rituals such as jiving, boasting, and toasting.[44] A speaker who asks listeners to join her in reciting a credo or a pledge they all know also is using ritual as a form of elaboration.

Sensory image.   Sensory images are words or phrases that communicate feelings and perceptions through one or more of the five senses—sight, smell, sound, taste, and touch. Author Barbara Kingsolver used olfactory images to help capture the idea of a rainstorm: "That was when we smelled the rain. It was so strong it seemed like more than just a smell. . . . I don't know how a person could ever describe that scent. It certainly wasn't sour, but it wasn't sweet either, not like a flower. 'Pungent' is the word Estevan used. I would have said 'clean.' To my mind it was like nothing so much as a wonderfully clean, scrubbed pine floor."[45]

Song. When a speaker sings a song or asks the audience to join in the singing of a song, an idea can be elaborated in a particularly vivid and powerful way. A speaker might ask an audience to join in the singing of "Joe Hill" to remind union workers of the strength and tenacity of labor, for example. Likewise, "We Shall Overcome" often is sung by an individual or by everyone present at civil rights events to suggest the perseverance and determination of those involved in the struggle to achieve equal rights.

Statistics. Statistics are numerical data designed to show relationships between or among phenomena. The relationship expressed can emphasize size or magnitude, establish trends such as increases or decreases in a particular population, or make comparisons. In a presentation at The Center for Substance Abuse Prevention, Antonia C. Novello, Surgeon General of the United States, used statistics to develop the idea that cigarette advertising expenditures have increased: "*In the United States, the tobacco industry spend [sic] nearly $4 billion in 1990 on product advertising and promotion.* This represents an increase of $376 million, or 10 percent, from the tobacco industry's advertising expenditures for 1989."[46]

Testimony. Testimony is the use of statements by others—either quoted or paraphrased—to elaborate on an idea. Testimony may draw its effectiveness from the content of the quotation or from the reputation or expertise of the person who is quoted. Shirley Witt Hill of the United States Commission on Civil Rights used the testimony of other Native American women to communicate the experience of Native women in the white world:

> But what are their perceptions of Anglo men and women? The White world into which Indian women foray for training and work is [an] often hostile, always confusing universe. Connie Uri (Choctaw/Cherokee) is frank about her perceptions of that world. She says that:

> "Racism has stood in my way in my career. To be female and Indian gives you a double bind. In medical school, the first

day of anatomy the teacher told me I wasn't worth teaching and he wouldn't do it. The medical school was segregated, two blacks, two Jews, two women, and we were all put at one end of the laboratory to work on cadavers. The lab assistants had to help us since the teacher refused to.''[47]

Tonal semantics.   Tonal semantics is the use of words and phrases chosen for their sound effects. In this form of elaboration, the sounds of the words develop the idea the speaker is conveying; the meanings of the words are less important and may or may not make sense. Many forms of elaboration rely to some degree on the sounds of words—alliteration and repetition, for example. But in tonal semantics, the sound of the words is emphasized more than the content. Forms of tonal semantics include:

1. Rhyme.   Rhyme involves the correspondence of words with one another in end sounds. Rhymes may form semantically meaningful words or may be nonsense rhymes. Jesse Jackson provided an example of rhyme when he said, ''Jesus said that we should not be judged by the bark we wear but by the fruit that we bear.''[48]

2. Rhythm.   Rhythm is the arrangement of words to achieve a regular recurrence of beat or accent. Jesse Jackson used rhythm in his speech to the Democratic national convention in 1984:

   I told them in every slum, there are two sides. When I see a broken window, that's the slummy side. Train that youth to be glazier, that's the sunny side. When I see a missing brick, that's the slummy side. Let that child in the union, and become a brickmason, and build, that's the sunny side. When I see a missing door, that's the slummy side. When I see the vulgar words and hieroglyphics of destitution on the walls, that's the slummy side. Train some youth to be a painter, an artist—that's the sunny side.[49]

Understatement.   In understatement, the speaker states an important point in a restrained style so that the low-key nature of the form is counter to the importance of the content it conveys. Holden Caufield, the protagonist in *The Catcher in the Rye*, used understatement in his announcement, '' 'It isn't very serious. I have this tiny little tumor on the brain.' ''[50]

This list provides some suggestions for ways in which the ideas of your presentation may be elaborated. Your own inventive processes will generate others as you work to form your presentation. The next step in the forming process is disclosing the form you have developed to your audience.

Chapter Seven

Disclosing Form

Disclosing form is the revelation of the form of your ideas to the audience. It involves all of the ways in which you communicate to your audience how you see the form of your presentation. The form you have created is "the organization of an entire personal world,"[51] as Umberto Eco puts it, and your task now is to communicate that world to the audience.

You cannot assume that your listeners will grasp the form you see so clearly. As your listeners decode your messages, they are engaged in a number of processes that work against their coming to the same understanding of your form that you have. They are forgetting much of what you say simply because the short-term memory can handle only a limited number of new inputs at one time. They are consolidating information into manageable and retainable chunks. They are fitting your new information into a context or framework with which they are already familiar, and it may not be the one you envision. They are developing expectations and making predictions about what will come next in your presentation. They are drawing inferences or developing new ideas from the ideas you discuss. In general, then, they are hard at work using your ideas to build an idea structure of their own. If your presentation does not help them build that structure, what they construct may have little resemblance to your own. You can increase the possibility of a common structure by providing explicit cues or structural hooks about your form to your audience.

Some cues are designed to alert listeners to the grand or global form of your presentation—its major ideas and the relationships you see among them. One way to guide your listeners toward an understanding of your global form is by making your commitment statement explicit during your presentation. This does not mean you have to give your commitment statement at the beginning of your presentation. You may choose, for all sorts of reasons, not to feature it from the beginning; you may want to save it for later in the presentation and develop ideas that move progressively toward it. In some presentations, an explicit statement of your commitment is not appropriate at all, of course, but in those where it is, a clear statement somewhere in the presentation is useful to the audience.

Other ways are available for disclosing your presentation's structure. A clear organizational format is useful as a cue of your form to your audience. Standard organizational patterns will be most familiar to listeners, but you will not always want to use conventional formats; often, ones of your own creation afford the greatest possibility of transformation precisely because they are distinctive. But whatever structure you choose, make sure you reveal it to your listeners and develop it sufficiently so its features are clear. You also will want to guide your audience through your form by distinguishing your major from your minor ideas so your listeners will be encouraged to retain the ones you see as most important.

Previews provide other excellent ways for letting your audience know how you conceptualize the structure of your ideas. At times, you may want to preview the entire structure of your presentation; you also may want to preview the steps you will use to develop a particular idea. The introduction of your presentation is another way in which you preview your form for your audience. Among the ways in which to introduce your presentation are:

Narrative.   In a narrative that functions as an introduction, a particular incident is described, with the speaker furnishing specific details about the characters, actions, and setting involved. Peggy Dersch, a student at Southeast Missouri State University, began a presentation on ignorance about rape with the following story:

> It was winter, 1976. A news item concerning the attempted rape of an eight-year-old child was reported on WABC-TV in New York City. Following the news, the station's weather announcer, Tex Antoine, began his report by reminding viewers of what he called an ancient proverb: "Confucius once say: If rape is inevitable, relax and enjoy it!" After enough protest calls, station officials required Antoine to offer a public apology. He said simply, "I regret making the statement." And then he added, "I didn't realize the victim was a child."[52]

Poem.   Just as poetry can be a form of elaboration, so it can be used to introduce a presentation. The concentrated imagery and rhythmic use of language combine to evoke a powerful introduction to the main idea of the presentation. A speaker discussing the silencing of women might begin a presentation with a portion of a poem by Marge Piercy called "Unlearning to Not Speak":

> Phrases of men who lectured her
> drift and rustle in piles:
> Why don't you speak up?
> Why are you shouting?
> You have the wrong answer,
> wrong line, wrong face.
> They tell her she is womb-man,
> babymachine, mirror image, toy,
> earth mother and penis-poor,
> a dish of synthetic strawberry ice cream
> rapidly melting.
> She grunts to a halt.
> She must learn again to speak

starting with I
starting with We
starting as the infant does
with her own true hunger
and pleasure
and rage.[53]

Question. An introduction can consist of a rhetorical question that the audience is expected to answer either mentally or out loud. A welcoming presentation to camp counselors, for example, could begin with this series of rhetorical questions:

So why do we do it?
What *good* is it?
Does it teach you anything?
Like determination? invention? improvisation?
Foresight? hindsight?
Love?
Art? music? religion?
Strength or patience or accuracy or quickness or tolerance or
Which wood will burn and how long is a day and how far is a
   mile
And how delicious is water and smoky green pea soup?
And how to rely
On your
Self?[54]

Quotation. In a quotation, a passage or statement made by another provides an eloquent preview of the speaker's subject. Business consultant Melodie Lancaster, speaking to the American Business Women's Association in Houston, Texas, started with a quotation: "I'd like to begin with a quote from Charles Handy's book, *The Age of Unreason*, which strikes at the heart of what I'd like you to remember today, 'The future we predict today isn't inevitable,' he writes. 'We can influence it if we know what we want it to be. . . . We can take charge of our own destinies in a time of change.'"[55]

Reference to occasion, audience, or speaker. Remarks that mention the occasion, audience, or speaker are frequent introductory forms. Kim Woo Choong, chair of the Daewoo Group, chose a reference to the occasion as the opening for a presentation:

Let me extend to you all my heartfelt congratulations in establishing the Southern California Chapter of the Korea-America Friendship Society. And I am deeply honored to have been invited to speak today at this, the inaugural meeting of the Chapter. I sincerely hope that the Chapter will make tremendous contributions to cooperation and friendship between the United

States and Korea, and I look forward to your efforts in this quest.[56]

English professor Karen Carlton used a reference to herself to begin a commencement address: "Exactly 30 years ago, I graduated from a small, liberal arts college in southwest Texas and prepared to live in a world I knew and understood. Roles were defined for me: I was engaged to be married; I would teach school so that my young husband could proceed with his studies; we would have children and live happily, safely ever after."[57] (Her complete address is one of the sample presentations included at the end of this book.)

Reference to previous speaker. In an introduction that refers to the previous speaker, the speaker recalls a major idea developed by someone else earlier in the interaction. That idea then is related to the ideas the speaker will develop in the presentation. A speaker might preface his explanation of a smoking policy, for example, by referring to a previous comment about the need for concrete solutions to conflicts over smoking in the office.

Notice that these introductions do more than simply preview the form of the presentation. They also preview the general attitude of the speaker toward the subject, the audience, and herself. In addition, they preview the tone of the presentation; it might be one of humility, arrogance, equality, openness, or warmth, for example. The tone established in the introduction provides immediate cues to the audience about the likelihood that the interaction will be one of safety, value, freedom, and openness.

You may have been told that introductions should be dramatic and exciting to catch the attention of audience members or to give them a reason to listen to you. Use of such a technique in the introduction is rarely necessary; your audience members have joined you in the interaction because they are interested in the subject and are seeking to fulfill interactional goals that are important to them.

Not only previews but summaries of your ideas constitute cues for the listeners as to the overall form of your presentation. These summaries may be brief overviews that follow elaboration of a major idea and can be used often throughout the presentation. The conclusion of your presentation also constitutes such a summary. Conclusions may assume a variety of forms:

Call to action. With some interactional goals, a challenge to the audience to take some kind of action may provide an appropriate summary. Publisher George C. Fraser, speaking to the Cleveland Teachers Union Home Learning Workshop, challenged his audience at the beginning of his conclusion:

I am throwing the gauntlet down and asking each of you for a *commitment* to do more. Now!

—To become indispensable.

—To vertically network by reaching down and lifting up and

—To reach back and pull forward.[58]

Narrative. Just as a story can introduce a presentation, elaborate on an idea, or serve as an organizational pattern, so it can provide a summary for a presentation. In her address to Americans for Democratic Action, Eleanor Roosevelt used a story to emphasize her main point:

> I was speaking to a little group of college students the other day who had started an organization where they tried to live the ideals of democracy, and one of them said to me, "I graduate this year. What do I do when I go home?" And I said, "You find people who feel as you do." He said, "I don't know any, where I live." Now, that shouldn't happen to any young person, because they should be sure that if they were really trying to live their convictions they would find support in their community.[59]

Pledge. Promising or agreeing to undertake certain actions constitutes a pledge; ending in this fashion often signals a speaker's commitment to a proposal or cause. Chief Dan George of the Coast Salish tribe ended his presentation commemorating Canada's 100th birthday with a pledge: "Oh, God! Like the Thunderbird of old I shall rise again out of the sea; I shall grab the instruments of the white man's success—his education, his skills, and with these new tools I shall build my race into the proudest segment of your society. Before I follow the great Chiefs who have gone before us, oh Canada, I shall see these things come to pass."[60]

Quotation. An eloquent statement made by someone else may be used as a conclusion, just as it can be used as an introduction. Congressional representative Barbara Jordan ended her 1976 Democratic national convention keynote address with a quotation from Abraham Lincoln: "Well I am going to close my speech by quoting a Republican President and I ask you that as you listen to these words of Abraham Lincoln, relate them to the concept of a national community in which every last one of us participates: 'As I would not be a slave, so I would not be a master.' This expresses my idea of Democracy. Whatever differs from this, to the extent of the difference is no Democracy."[61]

Reference to occasion, audience, or speaker. A presentation can be concluded by remarks about the situation, audience, or self that remind audience members of the main idea. In a commencement address to the California Western School of Law, Richard W. Carlson, director of Voice of America, closed with a reference to the audience:

> To you may be given the opportunity either to nurture or snuff out the germinating seed of information accessibility. All of us, in fact, have a role to play in ensuring that decades from now an informed public worldwide will have the opportunity to play an increasingly significant role in world affairs. The legal boundaries that people like you help to establish may make the difference between a world in which democratic principles are held high and one in which exploitation and misery are the norm. I know you are up to the challenge. Thank you.[62]

Reference to opening. A reference back to the opening of a presentation provides a sense of completeness to the main ideas developed. Christine D. Keen, issues manager for the Society for Human Resource Management, began a presentation with a reference to a Chinese proverb: "The Chinese have a curse: 'May you live in interesting times.' And these certainly are interesting times. American business and American society are undergoing dramatic changes, and human resources sits right at the crossroads of these changes." To close, she referred back to her opening proverb: "For at least the next decade, then, we will all live in interesting times. And it's up to us to determine if that's a curse or a blessing."[63]

Summary of main idea. In a conclusion that summarizes the main idea, the primary idea of the presentation is emphasized. George C. Fraser followed his call to action with a restatement of the theme of his presentation: "In closing, ladies and gentlemen, I say to you once again: We must redefine the meaning of life. Life is about happiness and happiness includes the self respect that comes from accepting responsibility for one's life and earning one's way in the world. We have all the tools we need, right here, right now."[64]

Summary of main ideas. Not just the overall theme of the presentation but the major ideas are reiterated in a summary of main ideas. Communication professor Richard L. Weaver II concluded a presentation on self-motivation with a summary of his main ideas:

> Several things, now, should be clear to you. First, self-motivation is directly related to stress-reduction. Second, stress is not always negative. Third, we are the makers of our own stress; thus, we *can* control it. Fourth, there are some useful workable techniques for controlling it. . . . Self-motivation is most likely to occur when we can successfully deal with the stresses in our lives. Your personal advance hinges on effort—your willingness

to put into practice techniques for activating or freeing the spirit.[65]

Your conclusion represents your last chance to communicate your overall vision of your presentation. Its primary function should be to reemphasize your main idea; thus, this is not the place to introduce new ideas that will detract from audience members' understanding of your central notion. The conclusion also needs to be consistent with the tenor of the rest of the presentation to enact in tone the qualities and conditions you have been seeking to engender in your presentation.

There is yet another function the conclusion should serve. It should convey to the audience what you would like to have happen next in the interaction. If you are giving a formal presentation to audience members with whom you are not likely to interact again, you will want to conclude in a way that signals the definite end of the interaction. Close with a sentence that leaves no doubt that the presentation is finished—a quotation, for example—and deliver the conclusion confidently to reinforce its finality. If you want to encourage participation by audience members following your presentation, you will want to signal that now is the time for them to speak with a conclusion that is more open, tentative, and invitational in character.

Cues such as introductions and conclusions point listeners to the global form of your presentation. Other cues reveal component parts of your presentation. These cues guide your listeners as you move from one idea to another or from an idea to its elaboration. Restatement or repetition, in which you repeat an idea, is one such cue. Transitions also work in this way. A transition is a sentence or several sentences that summarize where you have been and preview where you are going in the presentation. "Because a local baseball team has a substantial economic impact on our city, the San Francisco Giants deserve our support" is a transition that would move you from a discussion of the economic importance of baseball, which you just completed, to talking about why the Giants deserve to be supported, the next point you will discuss in your presentation.

The processes of focusing, constructing connections, and elaborating, in which you are engaged as you form your presentation, also are processes in which your audience members engage as they listen to your presentation. From the first bits of information they hear from you, they begin to construct hypotheses about the form of your presentation. They attempt to discover your focus, they construct relationships linking your key concepts to one another, and they use your forms of elaboration to determine and understand your important points. As you incorporate into your presentation explicit cues for the audience about these aspects of your presentation—as you disclose your form—you make these processes easier for your listeners and encourage them to reach conclusions similar to yours about the nature of your presentation's structure.

Chapter Eight

Making
Plans

A t the end of the process of forming your presentation through focusing, constructing connections, elaborating ideas, and disclosing your form, you are ready to prepare a speaking plan and the notes from which you will speak. A speaking plan is a summary of the major decisions you have made about your presentation. At this point, your plan still may be tentative and fragmented, but it is an approximate representation of your understanding of your presentation in some kind of verbal form. One way to think of it is as a path you have chosen to take through your understanding of your ideas.

You probably will want your speaking plan to include information about these elements:

Audience.   Identify your audience.

Setting.   Identify the setting for your presentation.

Interactional goal.   State your interactional goal for the presentation. To assert identity? To build community? To articulate a perspective? To secure adherence? To discover knowledge and belief?

Commitment statement.   Write a commitment statement that captures the initial assertion you will develop in the presentation.

Major ideas.   State the major ideas you will develop in the presentation. This section is the most extensive part of your speaking plan, for here you include the major ideas and primary supporting ideas of your presentation. Many different formats exist for depicting the major ideas and the relationships among them. One way is to outline them. Translate your major and minor ideas into key words or phrases and arrange them hierarchically in groups of points and subpoints. Your major ideas are major headings, and the elaborations of them—the minor ideas—are subpoints under them in the outline.

Sometimes, you will find that an outline form cannot capture adequately the vision you have for your presentation because an outline requires that your ideas be structured in a linear, hierarchical way that limits and constrains your subject and your approach to it. In such cases, a visual diagram will serve you better than an outline to present the major ideas, their elaborations, and the relationships among them. A visual diagram involves summarizing your major ideas with key words and phrases and laying them out in the structure in which you see them related. Lines and arrows indicate the relationships among the major ideas.

Organizational pattern.   State the organizational pattern your major ideas assume.

Major forms of elaboration. List the names of the forms of elaboration you use to develop your major ideas.

Introduction and conclusion. Although a speaking plan is not detailed enough to allow you to show all of the ways in which you provide cues to your audience concerning your order, you can indicate the kind of introduction and conclusion you are planning, thus indicating major ways in which you plan to preview and summarize your ideas.

Below are two sample speaking plans, showing the two different styles of presenting the major ideas—an outline and a visual diagram. Both of the presentations summarized in these speaking plans are included in the sample presentations at the end of the book.

Speaking Plan for "Who Is a True Friend?"

Christa C. Porter

1. **Audience.** High-school students
2. **Setting.** Sunday-school class
3. **Interactional goals.** To discover knowledge and belief; to articulate a perspective
4. **Commitment statement.** Let's develop a definition of friendship and see in what ways God can be a friend.
5. **Major ideas:**
     I. Audience's perspectives on friendship
    II. Expanded definition of friendship
        A. My definition of friendship
            1. Someone who will respect what I say
            2. Someone who is there for me
        B. What the Bible says about friends
            1. Proverbs 18:24
            2. Proverbs 27:10
        C. How we can be true friends
            1. Keep secrets
            2. Be trustworthy
   III. God is a trustworthy friend
6. **Organizational pattern.** Rogerian
7. **Major forms of elaboration.** Audience participation, comparison and contrast, definition, discussion, exaggeration, example, questions

8. **Introduction.**   Reference to audience, question;
   Conclusion.   Summary of main idea

Speaking Plan for "The Coming Chill"

Sally Miller Gearhart

1. **Audience.**   Participants at a rally—many of them lesbians, gay men, and bisexuals—remembering the deaths of Harvey Milk and George Moscone
2. **Setting.**   Civic Center Plaza, San Francisco
3. **Interactional goal.**   To build community
4. **Commitment statement.**   With you [Harvey] as our model, we can meet the challenges of the coming chill.
5. **Major ideas:**

Bright spots:
1. Art Agnos mayor
2. Harry [Britt] head of Board of Supervisors
3. AIDS quilt
4. Lesbians, gay men, bisexuals coming out

We're not quitting:
1. Will not let San Francisco become another Navy town
2. Will not give in to conservatism
3. Will remind people of California of the values San Franciscans hold dear
4. Will come out
   A. As lesbians, gay men, bisexuals
   B. As liberals

Harvey, you gave us a model
for meeting the coming chill

Changed climate:
1. Community decimated by AIDS
2. Nuclear battleship coming to San Francisco
3. U.S. flag despised
4. Mother Earth reeling
5. Greatest tools of century in hands of rich and greedy
6. George Bush is President
7. Dan Quale is Vice President

Tasks confronting us:
1. Hold back the spill of blood
2. Keep abortion rights
3. Watchdog legislation
4. Halt pendulum's momentum

6. **Major forms of elaboration.** Comparison and contrast, example, explanation, metaphor, repetition
7. **Organizational pattern.**   Web
8. **Introduction.**   Reference to occasion and audience;
   Conclusion.   Pledge

Your speaking plan allows you to assess the results of your forming process and to discover whether they match up with the mental vision you have for your presentation. It also allows you to do a final check of whether the communicative options you have selected facilitate or impede the creation of an environment in which transformation may occur—whether they contribute to the creation of safety, value, freedom, and openness in the interaction. The following questions will help you decide if the various options you have planned for your presentation create or inhibit possibilities for transformation:

Audience. How carefully have you considered the characteristics of your audience members, their interest in this interaction, and their willingness to be changed as a result of it?

Setting. What have you done to minimize distracting environmental factors that might inhibit or negate your efforts at establishing the conditions of safety, freedom, value, and openness?

Interactional goal. Does your interactional goal promote the creation of conditions that maximize possibilities for transformation? If your audience members' interactional goals are at odds with creating a transformative environment, do you attempt to re-shape their expectations, encouraging them to join you in working to create such an environment?

Commitment statement. Do you convey to audience members your willingness to yield your tentative commitments as a result of your interaction with them? Do you suggest that you are willing to follow the interaction where it goes and to be transformed in the process? In communicating your commitment statement, do you suggest that you value the commitments of audience members if they are different from yours?

Major ideas. Do your major ideas communicate the essence of your perspective so that your audience members can understand it?

Organizational pattern. Does your organizational pattern open or restrict the terms of the interaction? Does it enable audience members to participate, if they wish, in the interaction? Do you provide sufficient unity and coherence in your presentation so your audience members can follow you without difficulty and understand your perspective easily?

Forms of elaboration. Do your forms of elaboration provide sufficient development of your ideas so your audience members are able to understand your perspective? Are your forms of elaboration relevant to the ideas they develop so the audience understands those ideas? Are the feelings you evoke through your choice of forms of elaboration ones that facilitate or impede the possibility of transformation? Do your forms of elaboration silence other participants because they are presented, for example, in technical jargon? Do the forms of elaboration you have chosen encompass sufficient variety so the audience remains interested in hearing about your perspective?

Introduction and conclusion. Do you provide sufficient cues about your organizational structure for your listeners in the introduction and conclusion so they can understand your perspective and enter the interaction without difficulty? Do the other cues you are planning for your presentation, such as transitions, provide a sense of order so audience members feel comfortable dealing with your perspective?

If a check of your speaking plan reveals any problems, this is the time to revise it. Do not be afraid to abandon the plan or parts of it and to create, if necessary, a new and better plan to guide your presentation.

Following completion and assessment of your speaking plan, you are ready to draft your presentation—to put it in the form from which you will speak. The format of your draft—notes, outline, or manuscript—will vary according to the mode of presentation you plan to use.

Three primary modes of presentation are available to you. In the manuscript mode, your presentation is written out completely, and you read it to your listeners. The advantages of this mode are that you will present your ideas in exactly the way you planned, using the precise language you intended. This style of presentation is one that will not allow you to "go blank" because every word is there, and it also insures a permanent record of the presentation.

A manuscript mode of presentation, however, has disadvantages, all of which serve as barriers to the creation of an environment in which transformation is likely to occur. One is that a complete manuscript is likely to be composed in a written style of language, which is more stilted and formal than the language you use in your natural, conversational, oral style. Another possible difficulty with the manuscript mode is that it requires that you read well. In fact, to deliver a manuscript presentation effectively, you must be able to read without letting your audience know you are reading, a skill many people lack. Finally, a manuscript mode of presentation does not encourage you to adapt to your audience during the presentation. Whatever happens in the course of the interaction—no matter how the audience is responding—you are likely to continue reading your manuscript because that is what you planned to do. Although the manuscript mode is not likely to be the usual mode of presentation you select because of its many disadvantages, there may be times when you feel you must use it. If you have a very strict time limit within which to speak, for example, you may want to use this mode to ensure that you stay within the time allotted.

When you choose a manuscript mode, you can make it work most effectively for you by careful attention to two processes. First, write in an oral style. After you have written your presentation, read it out loud and make sure it reads the way you speak. Change all the stilted constructions you never would use in speaking to ones you would use in conversation. Insert contractions such as *don't* and *wouldn't* in the place of *do not* and *would not*. Replace jargon or highly formal words with more ordinary, casual, and even slang words and phrases if they are part of your normal speaking style and are appropriate for your subject, audience, and occasion. The following is a sentence from a presentation by Peruvian author Mario Vargas Llosa that is more appropriate for a written than a spoken style: "The key question which one needs to respond to with technical and scientific arguments, and not just emotional or ethical ones, is the following: can these cultures become modern and overcome oppression while conserving what are essential or at least fundamental elements of the language, beliefs and traditions?"[66] A more conversational way of communicating this idea might be: "The key question we need to answer is: can these cultures become modern and overcome oppression while conserving essential elements of their language, beliefs, and traditions? We need to answer that question with technical and scientific arguments—not just emotional and ethical ones."

The second process necessary to achieve an oral style in a manuscript mode is practice. Read the presentation out loud, over and over again, as often as you can. Become so familiar with it that you rarely need to look down at your pages. Work on telling your material to your audience just as you would in a conversation. You need to be careful, however, that you do not sound memorized as you read the manuscript. Think about your ideas as you say them and remind yourself of the feelings and emotions that led you to express ideas in particular ways.

A mode of presentation you are likely to use more than the manuscript is the extemporaneous mode. In this mode, you speak from notes of some kind, and not everything you plan to say is written out. Each time you give the presentation, it will be different as you spontaneously create the presentation from your notes. This mode of presentation allows you to present your ideas in a well-thought-out and organized fashion but also to be conversational in tone and to adapt readily to the audience as you present your ideas. You still will want to practice a presentation delivered in this mode many times to ensure that your ideas are presented in ways that encourage your audience's interest and attention and do not detract from your ideas.

On some occasions, you will use a third mode of presentation—the impromptu mode. In this mode, you speak with little or no preparation, forming your presentation at the time that you speak. The result is a natural and spontaneous speaking style. This is a mode of presentation you use often. When you speak in class; offer your ideas at a staff meeting; or explain, in response to a question from your supervisor, how your current project is progressing, you are engaged in impromptu speaking.

If you have chosen either the manuscript or extemporaneous modes of presentation, now is the time to draft your manuscript or notes. If you are using the manuscript mode, write out your speech in a way that enables you to read it easily. Typing it double or triple spaced using a large font size is one way to assure readability. For the extemporaneous mode, create a set of notes in whatever format works for you. You may prefer a list of key ideas, words, and phrases that prompt you to recall your ideas and their forms of elaboration, or you may want to use a formal outline. Whatever the format, it may be written on notecards or full sheets of paper. You may find that the frequent shuffling of many notecards is distracting to you and your audience and that turning just a page or two of full pages is less so.

Your final step in the construction of your notes is to insert into them any reminders or cues about what you want to highlight or remember. Use a highlighter to mark your major ideas so you can locate them easily, for example. Feel free to make notes to yourself about any aspects of delivery you want to remember. If you tend to forget to breathe when you speak, for example, write *breathe* at various places in the margin. *Slow down* might be helpful to write at the tops of pages or notecards if you tend to speak fast when giving a presentation.

Most of the time and effort involved in creating presentations happens during the forming process. At this point, you have made decisions about focusing, constructing connections, elaborating ideas, and disclosing form. As a result, you have a speaking plan and a set of notes from which to speak.

Chapter Nine

Delivering the Presentation

The final step in the process of creating a presentation is the actual delivery of what you have prepared. Delivery is the use of your body to communicate the ideas you developed in the forming process. It involves such elements as posture, movement, gestures, facial expression, eye contact, voice, physical appearance, and clothing.

As is the case with all of your communicative options in the process of planning a presentation, the choices you make concerning delivery either contribute to or impede the possibility of transformation. Depending on the options for delivery you select, you either can help to create an environment in which growth and change can take place or one in which the possibility of transformation is stifled—one devoid of the conditions of safety, value, freedom, and openness.

The delivery of your presentation may contribute to the creation of the four conditions in various ways. They are more likely to be created, for example, with posture, gestures, and facial expressions that communicate warmth and a genuine interest in audience members rather than combativeness, aloofness, or superiority. A voice that is gentle and suggests friendliness is more likely to create a sense of safety and value for the audience than one that is intimidating and jarring.

Eye contact with the audience usually suggests that you sincerely want your audience members to understand your perspective; it also communicates respect for and interest in their responses to your perspective and in the perspectives they bring to the interaction. If your audience members are from cultures in which direct eye contact is regarded as insulting or as a lack of respect, however, efforts to create an environment in which they feel safe and valued would need to assume a different form from those in which direct eye contact is expected. You would need to position yourself so that direct eye contact with your audience is minimized—sitting in a circle, for example.

An environment of growth and change also is more likely to be created when you yourself feel comfortable as you are speaking—when you use gestures and movements that are natural to you. Scratching your head, putting your hand in a pocket, or bringing a fallen scarf up to your shoulder are not inappropriate to do while speaking if they relieve your own discomfort.

A second way in which delivery contributes to the possibility of transformation is that it provides additional means for you to represent your perspective fully. If you have thought carefully about and explored your perspective thoroughly and are convinced it has merit and ought to be included in the interaction of which you are a part, it deserves the best possible expression you can give it. The more attractive and appealing you make the perspective through your delivery, the more likely it will be accorded full consideration by others.

Elements of delivery offer various ways to give full expression to your perspective. Managing aspects of delivery that may be distracting for your audience is one way to ensure that your audience members focus on your message. Pacing back and forth throughout your presentation, placing and replacing your hands in a pocket, using vocal distractions such as *uh* and *you know*, or fanning your notecards, for example, may be distracting for your audience and divert their attention from the perspective you seek to communicate. A rate of speech that your audience can follow easily is another way to direct your audience to focus on your ideas.

Your physical appearance, clothing, jewelry, and hair style may enhance the attractiveness and appeal of your perspective by encouraging your audience to want to investigate and explore what you have to offer. These aspects of your appearance also may enact your perspective, nonverbally reinforcing or modeling the perspective you are presenting verbally, as when you wear a particular hairstyle, a certain color, or a token of identification associated with a perspective as you talk about it.

If you find you have difficulty creating an environment in which transformation can occur and giving full expression to your perspective through elements of delivery, you may suffer from communication anxiety or what is popularly called *stage fright*. You may find that you become nervous when you have primary responsibility for communicating in a situation—a nervousness that interferes with the creation of an atmosphere of safety, value, freedom, and openness and that detracts from your efforts to express your perspective. You may experience, for example, stuttering or stammering; trembling hands, knees, or voice; excessive perspiration; accelerated heartbeat; blushing; or a dry mouth.

You may feel communication anxiety for several legitimate reasons. One source of anxiety may stem from the fact that presentational speaking requires you to stand apart from the group and thus to have more attention focused on you than normally is the case. There is an expectation, when you are asked or choose to speak, that you will have given some thought to what you are about to say and that it will offer a perspective or viewpoint that, if not novel, is at least cogent and perhaps even interesting. Because you are primarily responsible for the communication in this situation, you may find the extra attention and close scrutiny unnerving and anxiety provoking.

A lack of preparation also may trigger feelings of anxiety. If you are not as ready as you would like to be for a speaking situation—you have not had adequate preparation time, did not know you would be asked to speak, or simply procrastinated in preparing your presentation—you probably will find yourself experiencing some anxiety. There may be times, too, when you are well prepared but still experience anxiety because of uncertainties related to your presentation. Perhaps you are planning a presentation with an interactional goal of discovering knowledge and belief. You have prepared fully for the discussion, but it is a mode with which you are uncomfortable and that generates anxiety for you. Perhaps your perspective itself is undergoing major shifts, and you feel a natural anxiety about articulating it, in its changing and tentative form, to an audience.

You also may feel anxious because you perceive you are in a hostile situation. Perhaps you know, from previous interactions with your audience members, that they feel as though they are competing with you or are threatened by you and seek to discredit you and your contributions. Perhaps they do not respect or value you because of prejudices they hold. In such speaking situations, the conditions of safety, value, freedom, and openness do not exist for you, and you have every right to feel nervous. You must create these conditions virtually from scratch and against many odds as you attempt to give voice to your perspective.

A fourth source of communication anxiety may be that you are offering a perspective alien to the speaking situation. You may fear owning your own words and taking a stand because your perspectives and ideas are not those sanctioned by and reflective of the mainstream. Your perspective may confront and disturb simply by offering another way of thinking or being. A presentation on Native American cosmology as a model for the corporate world or the effort to introduce feminist perspectives into a discussion are examples of these kinds of situations. You are not likely to win approval for your perspective in this situation, which may heighten your self-consciousness and thus your anxiety.

Yet another possible reason for experiencing communication anxiety is the feeling that you have nothing to contribute to the interaction. This feeling may be the result of having been silenced in the past, of feeling devalued in a group, or of not having the communication tools to express your perspective adequately. You do not believe that the perspective you have on the world is one that no one else has. You do not see it as unique—as something no one else is able to form and deliver as you do. You believe that others will articulate the perspective you would offer and see no particular reason to speak up yourself. If this is the case, a situation in which you are expected or asked to communicate is likely to generate anxiety because you will feel your contribution must be novel and different from the perspectives expressed by the others.

Although all of these sources of anxiety are legitimate, the anxiety that may impede your efforts to create an environment of growth and change can be managed. You may have been given all sorts of advice for dealing with communication anxiety; not all of it helps you create such an environment. You may have been told, for example, to look over the heads of your audience members; to imagine them sitting before you in their underwear; or to say over and over to yourself before you speak, "I'm a better person than they are." All of these techniques, however, create just the opposite conditions from the ones you are attempting to foster. They require you to see yourself as superior to your audience rather than as a participant in an interaction in which everyone's perspective is welcomed and valued. They also assume a generally hostile and inhospitable environment. Such an environment may not actually exist; if it does, your presentation can help to change that situation.

Some ways of managing communication anxiety do allow you to contribute to the creation of the conditions of safety, value, freedom, and openness. One way is simply to deal with the symptoms you tend to experience so your discomfort with or embarrassment about them does not interfere with your efforts to communicate. If your mouth tends to be dry when you speak, for example, bring water to sip throughout your presentation. If your neck turns red when you speak, wear a turtleneck or a scarf that covers it. If shakiness is your body's preferred symptom, try to engage in some physical activity before your presentation to rid your body of excess energy—take a walk, breathe deeply, or simply move your head and arms, for example. Once you know that you have addressed your body's symptoms of communication anxiety, you will feel more comfortable and can concentrate on creating the kind of environment you desire.

Communication anxiety also can be lessened through practicing your presentations, if they are the kinds of presentations for which you have some preparation time. Practicing your presentation out loud, in whatever body posture you will adopt in the actual situation—sitting, standing, or sitting on the floor, for example—will increase your level of comfort during the actual speaking situation. This kind of practice will give you a sense of how you will feel when you are talking without interruption for several minutes. Practicing as if it were the real thing also allows you to clarify your perspective—you may discover as you say your presentation out loud new insights about and connections among your ideas.

Voicing your perspective whenever you get the opportunity is another way to decrease communication anxiety. Whenever you are given the chance to present your ideas, take it. The first several or perhaps the first hundred times you accept the responsibility for being a primary communicator, you will be uncomfortable and will experience the symptoms of anxiety that are familiar to you. Gradually, however, they will begin to disappear. You will feel more comfortable with the process of presenting ideas orally, particularly as you find yourself in and help to create environments in which your words and those of others are valued. You will discover that you have good ideas to contribute and that others appreciate your input into the interaction. You even may reach a point where you begin to enjoy the experience of presenting ideas orally because of the insights you gain from the exchange of ideas and the possibilities for transformation that result.

The delivery of your presentation is the culmination of your invitation to transformation. Your delivery reflects the choices you have made in the forming process of inventing, planning, and developing your presentation. If your choices have contributed to the creation of safety, value, freedom, and openness, the interaction that results as your audience members respond to your invitation will enable everyone involved to consider changing in some ways. The result, we hope, will be further conversations that produce greater understanding, more creative solutions to problems, and ever more opportunities for transformation.

Sample
Presentations

Why I Am Still Black

William B. Allen
Commissioner of the United States Commission on Human Rights

Presented to
Grambling State University, Grambling, Louisiana,
February 20, 1991

*The "President Johnson" to whom William Allen refers
in the presentation is Joseph Johnson, then president
of Grambling State University. The reference to
Proposition 48 addresses the controversy over whether
the NCAA should establish minimum academic
standards for incoming college athletes. If those
standards (ACT or SAT scores plus high school GPA)
were not met, the students were prohibited from athletic
participation in the freshman year.*

Good Morning, President Johnson, guests, students, faculty, and
my niece, Treyonde Allen, who sits there among you somewhere.
I am very happy to be with you. I am especially happy because I
have long admired your president for the courageous battle he has
waged against the NCAA [National collegiate Athletic Association]
and, more importantly, in defense of us. For we do have to
remember those who defend us, both because they inspire us to
defend ourselves and because we owe them a continuing debt of
gratitude for pointing the way that we are able to follow.

I spent time this morning with Dr. Jones touring Grambling
State. It was [an] enormous pleasure because this beautiful plant
speaks so well of all your efforts and the seriousness with which
you pursue the educational enterprise.

I am encouraged this morning to think that, as a consequence of what has happened here these—I was going to say these last fourteen years, President Johnson, but you will excuse me, and I will say these—last ninety-one years, that this entire country will be the better as we move into the twenty-first century.

This morning I want to speak to you about a special topic, one that relates to the broad theme of Black History Month. My title is, "Why I Am Still Black." I thought I should talk about that because today it's a question today for so many of us—what we should call ourselves. I have continued to call myself black. I think from time to time I ought to explain why, to let people know what's going on.

Let us remember, as you doubtless do, how Carter G. Woodson originally created Negro History Month. It is not insignificant for us to bear in mind, the changes we've lived through as the decades unfold. Negro History Month has become for us Black History Month, and it wasn't by accident that it became so. Certain victories were achieved when Negro History Month became Black History Month—certain victories that I am very reluctant to give up—and, because of which, I think we all stand better off today, better able to present our case and to speak to the necessities of the United States at the end of the twentieth century.

We usually gather in February to celebrate Black History by going through the list of our heroes, and the list is long, happily— the distinguished names that we can recall, or who can fill our breasts with pride as we look back. But I've been reflecting in recent years that perhaps we need to do a little more than just to remember those distinguished names. In fact, I have had a personal experience that persuaded me of this.

One of the courses that I'm teaching this spring is Euclid's Geometry, at Harvey Mudd College. And, of course, Euclid's Geometry is just plain, old geometry. It's kind of hard to give it special political and moral significance in our time, nevertheless, Euclid was quite probably black, and he was, of course, an Alexandrian, living in that original and most successful of all multi-cultural societies. I reflected that, in this course which I at least think is an exciting course, I did not have a single black student enrolled. And that led me to remember that when I have taught my course in moral fables, in which the major reference is Aesop, who was arguably black, I also did not have a single, black student enrolled and I tried to come to terms with what that meant. And I thought, perhaps it means this—perhaps it means that we don't have to consult a long list of proved, or arguably black geniuses in order to establish a curriculum to follow. Perhaps it's totally irrelevant who signs up for what course. Perhaps it is far more important to know that we have entered into a path of education that is leading forward, not backwards.

Next, I thought back to a historical event that persuaded me still more of this, and encouraged me to adopt the theme I want to talk about this morning. I remember something about Benjamin Banneker that we don't often talk about. In fact, I've never heard anyone remind us of it, perhaps because it's, in some ways, a painful story. But, since Benjamin Banneker could be said to have been the first to initiate the struggle for civil rights for blacks in the United States, I think we ought to remember him.

Benjamin Banneker wrote a letter to Thomas Jefferson in 1791, just after Jefferson had become the first Secretary of State under the Constitution. In the letter to Jefferson, Banneker pleaded for his race. He asked the author of the Declaration of Independence to exert his influence, not only to remove slavery, but to remove all those indignities that black people undeservedly suffered in the United States. He held up the standard of the Declaration to Jefferson and said,

> If you really believe, now is the time to prove it.

In writing the letter, Banneker had also sent to Thomas Jefferson a copy of the almanac that he had just completed. Almanacs were a very common production in the 18th century. That is to say, people who had the learning often devoted themselves to the task of producing almanacs which would then end up in people's homes. Folk would refer to them day by day in order to know what the weather was. They didn't get morning weather reports the way we do from comical weathermen on the television set. Their television was the almanac. And usually, in order to produce an almanac, you had to have sufficient mathematical ability, including trigonometry, among other things, in order to be able to perform astronomical calculations. Banneker had just finished such an almanac and he enclosed that in the letter to Thomas Jefferson. Jefferson assumed that the almanac was sent by Banneker, along with his plea in behalf of Banneker's black brothers and sisters, in order to prove that black people were intelligent enough to be regarded as equals. So Jefferson looked at the evidence for Banneker's humanity, which was his almanac, his knowledge of trigonometry, his knowledge of history, and concluded that maybe, MAYBE this might be evidence of equality.

In the process, of course, what Jefferson was doing, was reminding himself and others of what he had done in his 1783 book, *Notes on the State of Virginia*. In that book Jefferson wondered out loud whether, in fact, black people really were human—whether there might not be some scientific test by which we could prove, once and for all, whether black people were human. In doing that,

Thomas Jefferson ran an enormous risk. He was very nearly seduced by the temptations of modern science, to abandon the moral ground on which the Declaration of Independence stood. For the Declaration of Independence does not admit any doubt about the question, who are human beings? It is our ability to recognize a human being as human, that gives the Declaration its value. To say that all men are created equal is also to say that every human being knows another human being when he sees one. When Jefferson started to flirt with the doubts of Rousseau, and of modern science, to entertain the notion that we can't be sure who is human and who is not, is to back away from the Declaration of Independence. Now, Jefferson was called on this by Joel Barlowe, the poet, who wrote to him and asked him to explain himself. In the course of his explanation he said about Benjamin Banneker, and Banneker's plea, and Banneker's almanac,

> Well, it seems to me that that is not final proof; this almanac
> is the work of a mind of very common stature indeed.

What that story tells us is the extent to which Benjamin Banneker, in order to fight for his people, had to submit himself to the undignified treatment of being submitted to Thomas Jefferson's microscope—Thomas Jefferson's humanizing microscope, if I may put it so.

And that raises a question, "Why should anyone EVER have to place himself in that position?" Is it necessary to defend your rights to invite people to call into question your humanity? And the answer is "no."

It was "no" in 1791 and it is "no" two hundred years later. It was "no" for Benjamin Banneker as he confronted Thomas Jefferson, just as it was "no" for President Johnson as he confronted the NCAA and its Proposition 48.

Now these reflections point to a practical difficulty with which we must deal. And that is the continuing question of how to remain self confident, how to remain secure within the knowledge one has of one's own abilities, while nevertheless navigating in the political and the social seas of the United States—the continuing struggle for equal rights.

Well, that is why I am still black. For it seems to me that until one can raise the issue of color without having color become an issue, the battle is not done. The war is not finished. To run from the issue of color, to substitute euphemisms for color will not do. Nothing short of complete and total victory will suffice.

I was reminded of this as I was reading words of some of the original representatives to the Congress of the United States from this area, that is, the original representatives of color—those who, in the aftermath of the War of American Union, were elected in the Reconstruction period and, who confronted directly this question of color, as they raised the standard of equal rights as one law for all Americans. I was inspired by the reflection that they always spoke unhesitatingly about color. And they were able to set forth with pride, a sense of accomplishment. They avoided every impulse to pander. They specifically said they wanted no favors. They were confident that, left to their own devices, with nothing stronger than the protection of the law, granting them the same status everyone else enjoyed, that they would succeed. And I, by the way, have confirmed their attitudes by my own experience and the evidence I've collected.

I've reminded myself that this school was founded in 1901 and that it was not alone. There are historically black colleges and universities throughout the south particularly, which sprang to life from a supposedly illiterate and ignorant people in the aftermath of the war. I say "supposedly" ignorant and illiterate advisedly, because it is obvious the ex-slaves were not ignorant and not simply illiterate.

It is obvious that, in the immediate aftermath of slavery, there was enormous progress, economically and educationally. There was a spirit of entrepreneurism. There was a development of mechanical arts and liberal arts, to a degree unparalleled in human history. And I remind you, by the way, that when the war ended, there were somewhere between three million and five million ex-slaves. That is to say, as many people as were in the United States at the time of the Revolution from Great Britain, when the United States was founded. But there was, in that short period of thirty years after the end of the war, a greater explosion in the development of schools and universities and enterprises, among those ex-slaves, than there had been at the end of the 18th century in the aftermath of the Revolutionary War. In short, it is perfectly clear that there was no need for anyone to adopt the ex-slave as a helpless child. And if the direct evidence doesn't make it clear, the indirect evidence cannot fail to do so. Because it wasn't until after the direct evidence had come in, that all those laws of Jim Crow came to be placed on the books—to chop off at the knees the sturdy oak that was growing so rapidly. It was the law that halted the progress of black people in America. It was not custom and tradition, it was not the legacy of slavery, the hangover of illiteracy or poor education; it was law. Pure and simple. They had to go so far as even to create separate drinking fountains and bathrooms in order to deny equal opportunity. To hold the freed people in check.

It has been proved in this country that black people are sufficient unto themselves. Given untrammelled opportunities, the obstacles of law removed, there is no denying the capacity for progress. And when you take that evidence into account, then you realize that there is a false argument abroad in the land, which we need to confront. The false argument is that we have spent one hundred years seeking to recover from the effects of slavery and, if we could only have a hundred years more of patient concern, of tutelage, then maybe we'll succeed.

The only thing from which black people of America have ever suffered is tutelage. The one thing from which black people of America most need to be free is tutelage. We are not children in their nonage, barbarians waiting to be introduced to civilization. By the same token, we are not aliens, we are not foreigners. We belong in these United States.

I want to share with you the perspective of one South Carolina member of the House of Representatives, speaking in 1874 in response to the request from another member of the House of Representatives that, instead of passing the Civil Rights Bill, the United States should simply help the ex-slaves to return to Africa. I want to share with you his response to that request to return to Africa because I think it speaks immediately to us today. This is what Richard H. Caine had to say. He said,

> The gentleman wishes that we should prepare ourselves to go to Africa, or to the West Indies, or anywhere else. I want to enunciate this doctrine upon this floor. You have brought us here and here we are going to stay. We are not going one foot, or one inch from this land. Our mothers and our fathers and our grandfathers, and our great grandfathers have died here. Here we have sweated, here have toiled, here we have made this country great and rich by our labor and toil. It is the aim of you now to want to drive us away after having taken all our toil for 200 years. Just think of the magnitude of these gentlemen's hearts, after having taken all our toil for 200 years, after having sold our wives and children like so many cattle in the shambles, after having raised cotton on our labors, after we have made their rice fields wave with abundant harvest, while they were fighting against the government and keeping us in bondage, now we are free, they want us to go away. Shame on you.

There is no escaping, it seems to me, the reality that what defines the black presence in the United States is precisely that it is present in the United States. There have been dark, dark days in the history of our people. But I want to tell you I see far greater triumphs in that history. The darkness is dark enough to be sure, but my mind's eye settles upon the nobility, the dignity, and the triumphs.

I am still black. I don't perceive a need to be otherwise. Most

American blacks agree with me, according to a new poll from the Joint Center for Political and Economic Studies. Only 15 percent of persons interviewed chose "African-American" as a preferred designation, while 72 percent preferred "black." I am very much aware of what kind of victory it was in the 1960s when I became black, I hadn't been black before that, you see. Before then, I was Negro. And when I became black, I became black in the context of crying out, "Black is Beautiful." I became black in the context of calling for, demanding, black pride.

It was an exhilarating feeling to know, finally, that I was not to be defined by someone inimical to my happiness. It was also exhilarating to recognize that my color was not a stigma. Not a matter of shame. When I became black, I became black for good. And it occurred to me, what a wonderful liberating experience it was.

In my studies I have recognized how long in America there has been ambivalence about the question of color. I remember the famous Louisianan, Homer Adolphus Plessy, to whom we owe a great deal for participating in manufacturing that case, *Plessy vs. Ferguson*. Now we, of course, are not grateful for the results in the case. The result was the law "separate but equal." But the case did give us something to which we have clung ever since and which remains a beacon to us. And that was an extraordinary dissenting opinion by Justice Harlan. That was the dissenting opinion in which one found the expression, "The Constitution is color blind."

Now I want to tell you what Harlan meant by that because I think there has been some misunderstanding. There have been some people today who say, this language, "the Constitution is color blind," is just conservative symbols, it's conservative code words for a new racism. It's meant to deny black people having their say, having access to governmental remedies for all kinds of deprivations."

That is not what Justice Harlan meant. Justice Harlan had never heard of affirmative action, so he cannot be accused of being opposed to it. Here's what he said, this is what he did. He wrote an opinion about relationships between the races that was opposed to the majority opinion. And we can go back and read them and see how these people thought about these large questions. We can count in the opinions the very words that they used. We can see in the majority opinion, for example, that when reference to the ex-slaves is made, the language that is used most of the time is the word "colored." A few times it's the word "Negro." Never the word "black." Whereas in Justice Harlan's opinion, the one that says "the Constitution is color blind," you'll find that the word Justice Harlan used most often was "black." A few times, "negro," never "colored." That gives us reason to wonder—what does this man mean? He says the Constitution is color blind, but the first thing he sees about us is black. Well, here's what I think it means. I think it means Justice Harlan could see black without seeing a problem. I think that is what we have been trying to get to. We need to live in a country where people can see black without seeing a problem. And I mean by that all people, by the way, not only white people.

We need to live in a time and in a nation where the expression "black" is not a symbol for tensions, is not a code word or shorthand for deprivations, and where it does not mean poverty; where it does not come to be identified with all kinds of social disorder; where it is, in fact, nothing other than full recognition of the humanity of our fellows. That is acceptance. Some of us present ourselves through varying accidents. We all do. We all come in one shape or form or the other. We all have a look. But what is that look other than the spiritual embrace of humanity?

No, we cannot run from our look. Neither is there any ideological victory to be gained for substituting for our look, some other name.

Black History Month is not meant to be a month in which we dwell upon history. It is meant to be a month in which we learn how to shape the future. That is what I believe Carter G. Woodson wished. That is what I invite you to seek. And nowhere do we work so earnestly to shape the future as in our universities, as through our education. We all are differently talented, but there is not one of us whose talent cannot be perfected. To encourage the perfecting [of] our differing talents is the one thing we can give each other today that is of the greatest value.

Yet, to be sure, there are continuing legal struggles. You all are doubtlessly informed that the 1990 Civil Rights Act did not pass, but has been proposed anew in the form of the 1991 Civil Rights Act, and you probably wonder to some degree what meaning this has for you. I will tell you in all candor that I think some of it is overplayed. If you knew how many Civil Rights laws there were, it would probably bore you just to hear them listed. If you had to deal with the reality that most of us don't have the foggiest idea what we're entitled to, simply because there are so many laws that are contradictory, conflicting among themselves and that, by this point in history, offer general confusion. But it's possible to cut through the confusion. We can consult broad aims, broad principles in order to structure our expectations. One of the things we ought to bear in mind in looking at these Civil Rights laws, is the question, "What really works?" I can say that what really works is to leave people unopposed—unopposed in the attempt to perfect their talents. I think that is the most important thing we have to give.

One of the things I most regret about the 1990 Civil Rights Act was the compromise that put a limitation, a cap, a maximum, on compensatory and punitive damages for discrimination complaints. I hope the new Act will reintroduce damages without a limitation. I have long believed that allowing people to take their case to court, and to win in court full monetary justice for the injuries they suffer, is the best way to put a short end to discrimination in our society. I still believe that.

When the president vetoed the 1990 Civil Rights Act, he rejected compensatory and punitive damages, saying,

> I oppose these because it is a tort-like approach that I do not want to encourage, and I would rather encourage the administrative procedures in agencies like the EEOC, the Equal Employment Opportunity Commission.

And I'm here to tell you that the administrative procedures that we have become familiar with for twenty-five years have served mainly to retard justice, to delay justice, to impede people being properly recompensed for the injuries they have suffered. And I've always thought it ironic that those who seek to persuade us that they act in our interest do so by denying to us the opportunity— the opportunities I should say—that for over a thousand years have always been characteristic of Anglo-American jurisprudence.

I'll give you one example of what I mean by this and I think it will, for you, serve to explain the whole subject. In the twentieth century, there has not been a single lawsuit over segregation in schools that has produced, for the winning plaintiff, a monetary settlement, wherever the plaintiff has been black. Not one. There have been countless lawsuits, thousands of lawsuits, a great many of them won by the black plaintiffs. They've all resulted in various administrative orders—busing, consolidation, faculty exchanges, courts taking over the schools and administering them. Not one has simply written out a check and turned it over [to] the winning plaintiff.

By contrast, three years ago, in the state of Florida, there were three young children, the Ray children, who had been impermissibly segregated in the public schools. They sued. The school district settled their suit for $1.1 million. Now those children weren't black. Those children were infected with the human immunodeficiency virus, the AIDS virus. They received $1.1 million because they were segregated. And do you know what? Nowhere in the country since, have there been any complaints of children with AIDS being segregated in public schools. I wonder why!

I ask you, then, to reflect what would have happened if instead of having busing orders, people like Linda Brown had received checks for one million dollars. It is clear that some of the remedies for discrimination complaints in our society, while pretending, paternalistically, to aim for the good of black people have, rather, simply served to delay justice. And one of the reasons I insist we remain black, is because we have to insist that justice not be delayed. We must remove the various remedies which serve only as obstacles and which, therefore, by permitting people to hide behind race, to use race, to use special categories, refuse to acknowledge that what we really are, are individual, American citizens with just complaints, who ought to have the same kinds of settlements everybody else gets.

Justice Warren, when he wrote thc 1954 decision in the case, *Brown vs. Board of Education*, explained himself by saying, "that in the aftermath of slavery, practically all the ex-slaves were illiterate and uneducated." That became the reason for Justice Warren deciding that what we had to do was to educate these people before they could meaningfully receive equality.

What I'm suggesting to you is that there is no way to turn over to someone else the task of preparing people for equality. What you see being accomplished here at Grambling State University can be accomplished here only to the extent that it's not left for someone else to do. What we have to learn to do then, is to return into ourselves, and we have to use the examples from our past to encourage us to return into ourselves. To gather anew the moral strength, the courage, the will to persist on our own and to triumph by our just efforts.

It is no longer open to us, it seems to me, to expect some day in the future, when the past will look different. We no longer have title to expect from ourselves a change. Identifying with other folk outside of the United States is not going to resolve for us the problem in coming to terms with who we are, where we are.

Like Representative Caine, I am resolved that I am not going to move one inch from here. And what that means is not that I'm not going to travel, I like to travel like everyone else, and I fly around the world and love to visit places and see the ancient roots of all kinds of civilizations, but I am not going to move one inch from here in my consciousness.

We've discovered something in these United States which is invaluable. We've discovered how to defend the claim of humanity. And, having discovered that, we now have to proceed to that defense. I don't think we can accomplish that defense until we can accomplish the victory I've laid out this morning, namely, the victory of knowing that we live in a world, in a country, where people can see black, white and anything at all, without seeing a problem. Where people can refer to color because color is no longer an issue.

The reason I remain black is because I insist on being all-American.

Arcata Town Meeting

Testimony presented to
the Arcata City Council, Arcata, California,
January, 1991

*In response to the start of the Gulf War in January, 1991,
the Arcata City Council approved a resolution declaring
the city "a sanctuary for all persons who for moral,
ethical or religious reasons cannot participate in
military action." The public debate spurred by the
resolution prompted the Council to call a town meeting
at which citizens could express their views. The meeting
began with the Council's vote to rescind the resolution;
it ended with Council members agreeing to consider, at
their next meeting, whether or not to take future action
in regard to the war. Because no council member offered
a proposed resolution for the agenda, however, no
further formal action was taken. Selected excerpts from
the testimony are presented here.*

Victor Schaub [mayor]: Welcome to this special meeting of the
Arcata City Council. . . . This meeting has a special agenda. It is
an official meeting of the City Council, and the item on the agenda
is as follows: "Public discussion of resolution 901–49. Resolution
of the City Council of the city of Arcata to be a sanctuary for all
persons who for moral, ethical or religious reasons cannot participate in military action." The Council will make some comments
after which the meeting, the public-discussion part of the meeting,
will be facilitated by Mr. Bryan Gaynor, who is our city attorney.
There are set rules for how the discussion will proceed, and Mr.
Gaynor will announce those rules and explain them after we have
done some initial things here. . . . At this time, I will entertain
comments from the Council members before we proceed

with the discussion portion of the agenda. First, I'll call on Council member Pennisi.

Sam Pennisi: Thank you, Mr. Mayor. I've been doing a lot of soul searching, as I think many of us have been doing, and maybe many of you have been doing this week, I don't know. I've got a couple of comments that will be very brief that I'd like to express to you. A little bit of this I said on Saturday, but this is a different group, and I'd like to take this opportunity. This past week has not been pleasant for you or me, and I wish to apologize personally, as one Council member, for this conflict that we are in this evening. When the sanctuary resolution was passed, I honestly thought we were declaring that there should always be a place in our hearts during times of conscription and war for conscientious objectors and that we had hoped that a peaceful solution might still be achieved in the Gulf. We were only three hours into the war when our Council meeting started last time. Obviously, I was wrong. I think wording was a problem and other things, and I won't go into details here. That's what we're here to hear about tonight. I was also wrong in not demanding a public meeting or questioning the wisdom of deciding on this issue for our community at all. For these things, too, I offer my apologies. I want to take this opportunity to state my personal, absolute support for the men and women who have been asked to fight, and perhaps die, for a war in which this country has seen fit to participate. And I emphasize *this country*. It went through the UN resolution, it went through Congressional debate; in my lifetime, I've never been witness to that. If we learned anything from the Vietnam conflict, it is to clearly separate the people who must go to war from the civil policies that find a need for war. I trust any war protester can appreciate the need for this distinction, and I can't emphasize that distinction enough. The tragedy of this resolution, in my opinion, is that we've divided this community unnecessarily, and for my part in that, I, too, am sorry. I have some ideas that might guide future larger-than-Arcata issues, but I want to hear this meeting's input before I finalize these ideas and make specific proposals, and I thank you all for coming this evening.

Victor Schaub: I, too, wish to publicly acknowledge the error of having adopted this resolution—of taking any action, especially on an issue as important as this. We allow public discussion about what color to paint a water tank in somebody's neighborhood, and I acknowledge the error of not having allowed public discussion. I dare say that each of the Council members recognized this error Thursday morning, if not Wednesday night, before the barrage of phone calls and other contacts that we have received. However, I wish to call to mind the quote of John Kennedy regarding the Bay of Pigs when he said, "An error does not become a mistake until you refuse to admit it." And we're admitting the error that we did not allow public discussion.

I want to remind us all of the things that we have in common. We all, those who support the resolution and those who are opposed, we all condemn the actions of Saddam Hussein. We have that in common. We all support the well-being of our troops and the efforts they are required to undertake. We have that in common. And we all have the desire for peace. We know that. We all have that in common. The debate is over how best to achieve that. I would like tonight to be a positive experience for our community—a night in which we can learn that we can have public discussion about an issue as serious as this and that it can be constructive and that we can have this discussion in a peaceful manner. I think we have an opportunity to demonstrate to the larger community, of which we are a part, that the issues of war and peace can be discussed publicly and peacefully.

Now, since we have all acknowledged that it was inappropriate for us to take action without public discussion, it wouldn't seem inappropriate, to me at least, to wipe the slate clean and to start right now having a public discussion of war and peace. It wouldn't seem inappropriate at this time for the mayor to entertain a motion to facilitate the beginning of that process—of that public discussion—by entertaining a motion to rescind the resolution that is before us so that we can then conduct public discussion and make a decision as to whether or not to adopt this or some other resolution. So at this time, I will entertain a motion from any Council member who desires to make one.

Bob Ornelas: I move that we rescind the Arcata sanctuary resolution number 901–49.

Audience: [Cheers and applause]

Bob Ornelas: And that we provide the opportunity for this town to develop a statement regarding the Persian war.

Victor Schaub: Is there a second to the motion?

Sam Pennisi: I second it.

Victor Schaub: Okay, the motion has been made by Council member Ornelas to rescind resolution number 901–49 and to commence a public discussion of what, if any, statement to make concerning the Persian Gulf war, and the motion has been seconded by Council member Pennisi. Is there a need for further discussion? Are we ready to vote? All in favor say aye.

Council members: Aye.

Victor Schaub: The vote is unanimous. Okay, at this point, then, we will commence the process of public discussion on this issue. At the end of the discussion, we will make whatever decision that we can make given what is on the written and posted agenda. To facilitate this process, I'm going to turn the meeting over to Mr. Bryan Gaynor. Bryan.

Bryan Gaynor: Thank you, Mr. Mayor. First of all, a set of rules of conduct for conducting this meeting has been prepared for you, and they are available at the door. I hope that each of you has had an opportunity to pick up a set of these rules and has familiarized yourself with them. I want to ask if the people who are outside can hear me clearly. [Crowd noise is heard.] I'll take that for a yes. And we can hear you. So, these rules are intended to provide an atmosphere in which the diversity of opinion that is present in this room and outside this room can be expressed and heard by all the participants of this meeting. . . .

    If you would like to speak, and of course everyone is encouraged to speak, you must obtain at the door of this hall one of the color-coded cards. If you are an Arcata resident or an Arcata businessperson, you should obtain a yellow card. If you are not an Arcata resident or businessperson and you wish to speak, please obtain one of the red-colored cards. The reason for this is we wish to hear from everyone, but this is a city-of-Arcata issue and, accordingly, Arcata residents and businesspersons will be given priority. That is, they'll be allowed to speak first. This doesn't mean that others from outside of Arcata will not be allowed to speak. Rather, it's merely to reflect the priorities of the Council. . . .

    We're asking that people who intend to speak be in the line that is on the left-hand side of the hall from my perspective, the right-hand side of the hall from the perspective of you in the audience. We ask that 10 speakers be in line ready to make their comments. Accordingly, when you come to the microphone to speak, we ask that you state your name and the fact that you're a resident of Arcata, if that is the case, or otherwise if you're not, and that you also indicate what your speaker number is. That way, the next person will know that he or she should be ready to come to the microphone. We hope, by following these procedures, that we can move expeditiously and allow the maximum number of people to be heard. Each speaker will be allowed one opportunity to address the Council, and each speaker will be limited to three minutes. . . .

I want to point out to everyone that this meeting is going to be broadcast subject to a two-hour time delay on channel 31. A video repeat will occur on January 26, Saturday, at 1:00 P.M.; again on January 30, Wednesday, at 7:00 P.M.; and on February 2, Saturday, at 1:00 P.M. Please address your remarks to the City Council. Personal attacks and name calling are not appropriate, nor is the interruption of any speaker. Please follow these rules, and please let us hear your comments. . . . So, will the first speaker please identify himself?

Robert Thomas: Thank you, Mr. Gaynor. Mr. Chairman, fellow Council members. My name is Robert Thomas. I am a co-owner of Joe Costa Trucking. We are located in the city of Arcata, California. I'd just like to say that I've been a member of this community for the past 15 years. My wife's family has been here for almost a century. I'm sure there has never been an issue that has divided the community as deeply as the resolution that was passed last week. And I would like to commend the City Council for the position they've taken tonight, and I would just like to say that I hope that this never happens again. I've addressed many public forums recently but none with as serious implications as this one has had. I represent a company that has approximately 100 families in the Arcata community. Many of them have loved ones in the Middle East, and many of them feel very strongly about the support that we show and provide for those family members. My comments obviously are not what I intended them to be because of the action that was just taken by the City Council. But I can tell you this: an overwhelming number of phone calls came into the city during the past 5 or 6 days, 75 percent of which opposed the pass of the resolution. And I would just like to say, once again to reiterate, that I commend you for what you've done this evening, and I would hope that a resolution similar to the one you passed will never be passed again. Thank you very much.

Bill Hanley: I'm number 91. My name is Bill Hanley. I thank the Council and everybody for going for the sanctuary. I just think it's lame to be out killing people in this day and age when we're supposed to be leading the world and world leaders, and we can't come up with a damn idea, another way around this. The only way to do it is to kill somebody. It's stupidity, and I applaud the Council. I wish you didn't rescind the resolution, and I hope you come up with another one. I don't think everyone has had the chance to speak yet tonight, and I think you need another night of discussion. Thanks.

Elizabeth Comet: [Gives peace sign to audience before beginning to speak.] Hi, my name is Elizabeth Comet, and I live at 1227 Old Arcata Road, and I'm number 94. God, I'm really nervous. I think the question is no longer whether war is appropriate or correct or not. That doesn't make any difference any more. It's now a question of choice—the choice to kill, to fight a war when you're not sure why we are at war. My father was a Marine. My grandfather was a Flying Tiger in World War II, and I've seen what happens to people who fight in wars. Friends, to choose to fight in a war is a very serious decision. To see people die, to kill other human beings, is a very important decision, whether it's for your country or for whatever reason. It's a heavy decision to make. I don't think there's anybody ever who has the right to tell you whether you have to kill other people. We have a country where we kill people to show people who kill people that killing people is wrong. This country gives people the death penalty to show other people that killing people is wrong, and now we're telling you that you have the choice—you either kill or you go to jail. That's crazy. This is insane. I was talking to my friend before this war broke out about going to Costa Rica this summer, and it's something I've always wanted to do. It's my summer, it's what I want to do this summer, but you know what? Now that this war has broken out, I'm going to go to Costa Rica this summer, and if my friends are drafted, I don't think I'll ever come back because I could not feel proud to be a member of a country that tells you either to kill other people or you go to prison. That's crazy.

Ron Grace: Good evening, ladies and gentlemen, City Councilmen. My name is Ron Grace. I'm a business owner here in Arcata. I was a resident here in Arcata for about 7 years. I presently live in McKinleyville. I am a proud member of the Arcata volunteer fire department. I am a proud parent of two students who graduated from Arcata High. My son is currently in Saudi Arabia. Many people tonight have voiced their opinion on a lot of different issues, many of which are not the reason why we're here tonight. But the real reason we are here tonight is your actions taken last week. The objective of tonight's meeting is to decide if we should pass a resolution similar to the one the Humboldt County Board of Supervisors passed. You have offended a small group of radicals. I am pleased that you rescinded your resolution, but you must pass a resolution in support of our servicemen in the Gulf and all over the world. Two groups are here tonight, one that will be here in Arcata for a short period of time—students and activists. The other will be here a long time—businesspeople and long-time residents— the silent majority, as many have said tonight. So you must consider this in your discussion of further passing another resolution. I ask you to uphold your oath of office, support the U.S. President and the Congressional action, and support the will of the citizens of Arcata or resign.

Frank Hollyman: Thank you. Good evening. My name is Frank Hollyman. I've lived in Arcata for 24 years. I am proud to say that I am from Arcata, even though I do disagree with what the Council did, but I would like to say this: It's been a pleasure to be in Arcata. I think there's an even ground that we all need to seek here, but we all need to have voice in order to seek that even ground, and we weren't granted that, I don't believe, in this case. I don't want you to make decisions for me unless you have my input. I can't make that decision for you, but I do ask you to search your soul and come up with an answer that fits for you but, more importantly, fits for Arcata, the city whom you represent. As I've said before, I've grown up in Arcata, I'm proud of Arcata. I have two sons I am raising in Arcata, and I hope that when they reach the draft age, there isn't a draft. But if there is, I hope that they will find it in their hearts to go and defend their country as the people we have over there today are defending their country. I hope they get the support from their town, which hopefully at that time will be Arcata. I was a Marine. I'm proud to say I was a Marine, and if I get called upon, I will go—not that I really want to go. I don't want to kill anybody. I don't think anybody here wants that. I think everybody wants peace. But we also want representative government, and all I'm asking you is give us a chance to have that representation. I also applaud your efforts to rescind this bill or this ordinance number 901–49, and I ask that instead of tearing apart Arcata, it might be a good idea to listen a little more attentively before decisions such as this are made in the future. Thank you.

James Moray: My name is James Moray. I'm a very new resident of Arcata. I think we've had a lot of requests here tonight for the City Council to resign, and there have been a lot of people saying they're ashamed to be living in Arcata because of this resolution. I think that's really ridiculous and terrible. They did not cause this split and this conflict. George Bush did. This war did. This war is causing us to fight each other and not realize that we all need to uphold our right to make a choice and live and decide for ourselves what we want to do. The draft violates the right to choose. I understand the people who are objecting to the fact that the City Council might have made this resolution hastily without input from the public, but if you're concerned with the democratic ideal, you should be here in support of people's right to make a choice for themselves. There's a very basic choice, whether you want to go thousands of miles, be commanded by George Bush and kill people and possibly be killed. I mean that's a very basic decision there, and I can't imagine why a community so concerned with democracy wouldn't want people to have that choice. That's really all I have to say.

Shacoti Walsch: Hello, my name is Shacoti Walsch, and I am a resident of Arcata, a student, and a mother. I've heard a lot of different things tonight, and I really do not understand, after reading this resolution, what in the world you can possibly be sorry for. You should be proud of yourselves, and if it is a democratic process that is to be encouraged here tonight, then I ask that it truly be a democratic process. If it means taking a vote of every citizen of Arcata, then we take a vote, but democracy should not be outweighed by money and power again. I really ask that. One thing I keep hearing over and over again is that we all seem to be united on our right to freedom. I do look for the things that we can be united on. George Bush has convinced a good part of this country that we are in Iraq for freedom, but I want to ask you something. Search your minds and souls and look. Where were we when the students in China were shot down if this is over freedom? Where were we when 700 Black babies were killed one morning for their rights of freedom in South Africa? Where were we? This is not over freedom, unfortunately, but if we can be united on the right to freedom, let's bring the issue back home. In the Constitution, it says we have the right to the pursuit of life, liberty, and happiness—the freedom to pursue life, liberty, and happiness. How can any of us be happy killing another human being? That's murder. I applaud you with my heart and my mind and my whole being for being the forerunners of such a resolution. We live in a changing time, and it is time to drop the old blind patriotism and pull the truth out from within ourselves of what it means to be free human beings, and freedom means to have a choice of whether to go to war or not go to war. Remember, the draft takes away our freedom. Thank you.

City Planning as a Career
Andrea Armstrong
Student, Ohio State University

Presented to
a presentational speaking class, Ohio State University,
Columbus, Ohio, spring, 1993

In this presentation, Andrea Armstrong assumed the role of a city planner, speaking to first-grade students on career day.

Hi, I'm Ms. Armstrong, and I'm a city planner for the city of Columbus. I'd like to ask you a couple questions. Do any of you have a favorite city?

Student: Columbus.

Columbus? Anybody else?

Student: Chicago.

Chicago? Yes?

Student: Las Vegas.

What do you all like about Columbus, since that's where we're living right now?

Student: The zoo.

Student: I like the playgrounds.

Used by permission of Andrea Armstrong.

The playgrounds? Anything else?

Student: It doesn't take long to get anywhere.

Student: The fair.

The fair—the state fair. You like going to the fair? I like going to the fair, too.

OK, those are some of the things you like about Columbus, but a long time ago, cities weren't such nice places to be. There were a lot of factories, there was a lot of smoke, cities were crowded, and there weren't very many parks. Kids actually used to have to play in cemeteries because there weren't parks in their neighborhoods to play in—that was the only green space they could find. That was before planning. What planners try to do is to make places nicer for people. They make cities places where people want to live and want to be.

Planners try to make cities better in a lot of different ways. For instance, they try to decide where schools should be. They try to make sure that there are enough parks and playgrounds in neighborhoods for families and friends to play in. They have to make sure there are police and fire services for everyone in the city. They need to make sure that there are enough water lines and sewer lines. They have to make sure that buildings are built correctly.

City planners have to know a lot about a lot of things. They have to know about law because they have to know laws that affect where and how things can be built. City planners also have to be good public speakers because they have to explain ideas and plans to people. They need to be architects and engineers—they need to know how things are built and how they can be built. They need to be computer users; they use computers to figure things out. They need to be demographers—they need to know how to use numbers and statistics and to figure out how many people are in cities.

City planners also need to be map makers. I've brought along a few of the maps I use at work every day. These are the kinds of maps that planners use and make. The first map is an annexation map. Annexation is how a city grows—how it gets more land. The purple area in this map shows Columbus in 1900; that's all the bigger Columbus was in 1900. If any of you have a grandmother who is 93 years old, that's how big Columbus was when she was born. Today, Columbus is as big as all the areas that are colored on this map. Planners need to know this, and they need to be able to provide services in all these areas. They need to make sure that there are police, fire, water, and roads and everything for all this area.

Your school is in this area, near the river. City planners need to know where the flood plain is for the river. We have something called 100- and 500-year floods. That means that we have a 1-in-100 chance to get a flood or a 1-in-500 chance to get a flood, which means the river will go outside of its banks. We need to know this so we don't build in those flood plains—people lose their houses and belongings if they do. Ohio State University's campus is located right here. It is in part of the flood plain, so part of this land may flood. We need to know that ahead of time.

This map shows flight contours for the airport, which is west of town—Port Columbus Airport. Every line on here is how loud the noise is from the air traffic in the air. We need to know this because nobody wants to live within these noise contours because it's loud, it hurts our ears, it's not good for our health. We need to make sure we don't build in those areas—it's not good for us.

Finally, we need to know where fire stations are located in our city. We need to make sure that if your house catches on fire, there's a fire station nearby that will be able to put the fire out. All the red circles are Columbus fire stations.

There are planning issues going on now that you might have heard about in the news or from your parents. The Tuttle Crossing area is a planning issue in Columbus. This is a mall that's being developed on the north side of town. It involves city planners who are trying to do all the things necessary to make sure the mall is a nice place.

So, planners do a lot of different things in their jobs. They have to know a lot of different things. Planning is a good profession for people who are curious. So, if you're a curious person and like to do a lot of different things, planning might be a profession for you someday.

Our Lives, One Life
Karen A. Carlton
Professor of English, Humboldt State University

Presented at
commencement ceremonies for the College of Arts and Humanities,
Humboldt State University, Arcata, California, May 22, 1993

Exactly 30 years ago, I graduated from a small, liberal arts college
in southwest Texas and prepared to live in a world I knew and
understood. Roles were defined for me: I was engaged to be married;
I would teach school so that my young husband could proceed with
his studies; we would have children and live happily, safely ever
after. In my graduating class of 1963 there were no people of color.
All of my professors were men. Sexuality of any sort was a darkly
kept secret. There were no divorced couples amongst my friends
or even the parents of my friends. There were no single parents.
Few people I knew drank alcohol or experimented with drugs. And
the word "ecology" was yet to enter the vocabulary of common
people. You can see that my reality of 30 years ago was somewhat
different from your own today. As a middle class, white and female
American, I stepped into a world with social, racial and political
boundaries, into a world of absolutes where who was who and what
was what and right from wrong were clearly defined.

When my husband and I moved to San Francisco in 1964, you
can imagine what happened to us. The world seemed to turn upside
down and inside out. You who are parents and grandparents
remember the times: The Beatles, the Free speech and Civil Rights
Movements, the Vietnam War, Watts, Hippies, the assassinations,
Free Love, and drugs. I think that is when the boundaries of our
institutions and cultures began to dissolve, at least for me and
people like me. Definitions began to blur and structures seemed to
vanish. I felt then like I was in an old black-and-white movie which

Used by permission of Karen Carlton.

was suddenly losing its clear story line, its well developed characters, its predictable ending, its clean focus.

Today we all share a great metaphysical secret, if I may state it so simply: There are no boundaries in the universe. Boundaries are illusions, products not of reality but of the way we map and edit reality. We are reminded daily that we live in a global economy, a global village, that the borders of countries are porous. Money flows around the world in electronic impulses, faxes go everywhere, satellite dishes collect images from all over, and the tapes of revolution can be played at any time or place. All of our major, social issues transcend national lines: AIDS, arms control, terrorism, the environment. As we well know in Humboldt county, the lumber mills of one country, with their emissions that produce acid rain, can denude the trees of the next.

Personal boundaries have dissolved, too. Many of you graduates cannot do as I did 30 years ago after my graduation ceremony, when friends and family socialized. Not all of you can say simply, "These are my parents" or "These are my brothers and sisters" or "This is my fiance." Many of you have step parents and step siblings, half brothers and sisters, parents of the same gender, or parents who have no biological relationship to you at all. Some of you are married or engaged to the person you live with, many of you are not; some of you are in love with people of the same sex; some of you are single parents; some of you are hermits who live in the woods. And none of this surprises any of us today because we, in the West, have forever moved from that prescriptive age where roles, behaviors and thoughts were fixed by societal norms and expectations.

So much good has come from the dissolution of these imagined boundaries. And so much fear. How exhilarating it is for women and people of color to move into areas so long monopolized by white men! And yet how lonely it is to assume new freedoms and territories without the familiar surroundings, the constant support, the comforting structures of old ways. How liberating it is to choose one's lifestyle, one's family and community, to enjoy the mobility of modern work and leisure. And yet how terrifying and even dangerous it often is to challenge or reshape the traditions of our past. How important it is to be aware of the interrelationships of ideas and organisms, to know, as the Tewa Indians say in one of their prayers, that "your life is my life; our life is one life." And yet how hard this is to remember and feel and *live* when races or religions or genders clash. Complexity, chaos, transformation— these are the watchwords of this day.

The question that presses upon all of us is this: With no boundaries, what will shape and contain our selves, our souls?

Without the benefit of authoritarian leadership, without the guidance of old and established institutions, without the forced structures of culture, economics, class, and gender, how will we know who we are and how to be? These are questions, I think, which a university education, particularly a liberal arts education, attempts to address. During your years at HSU, you graduates have been in an environment which has allowed you both the freedom and safety to explore various ways of thinking, being, living. The place of the university, the faculty and staff and friends surrounding you, have permitted many of the benefits and postponed some of the hazards of living with no boundaries.

But now you are leaving this place of wholeness (for that is what a university is: a unified whole) and commencing another life. Outside these halls and this ground, you will have to make your own internal boundaries, forge your own selective communities, establish your own moral order. What will they be? Who will you be? I have a pretty good idea, for I've been watching you, working with many of you, learning with all of you. The German poet Rilke wrote, "The future enters into us, in order to transform itself in us, long before it happens." Your future is in you now, in the choices you have made these last few years at Humboldt State University, in the books you've read, in the papers you've written, in the speeches you've made, in the people you've met, and in the actions you've taken. You have been creating the selves and souls that will endure and even embrace the complexity, chaos and terrible freedom of a universe without boundaries. You've been making yourselves and the future.

Here is a short, short story: Once a group of men and their captain faced a large, terrifying, and unpredictable beast. The men pressed upon the captain and said, "What course of action shall we take?" The captain hesitated to answer at first and then said judiciously: "I think I shall praise it." While I am no captain, I believe it is true that the future is large, terrifying, and unpredictable—that without you and your best selves, it will be a beast.

So just to be safe, let me, for a minute, praise you. Let me act as a mirror and reflect back to you the selves, the souls, and therefore the future I have seen you making: You are generous, compassionate people, devoted to justice and to the well-being of those less privileged than yourselves. Rather than seeking individual power, you work for the empowerment of all. I know that many of you give all together hundreds of hours each week to helping and educating children, young adults, refugees, the homeless, and neglected and abused people. You value collaboration and cooperation; you resist dualism even as you embrace paradox. By celebrating a multidimensional and multicultural view of the world, you recognize and challenge the awful readiness innate within each one of us to fear difference and opposition. You are lovers of the earth and through personal and collective actions you move against ecological destruction. I watch you write essays on recycled paper, and carry your mugs to The Depot for coffee. I hear you call plants, animals and stars by their particular names. You are makers of art, in the service of beauty, interested in creating knowledge as well as acquiring it. You seek ways of knowing which include feeling and being as well as thinking. By holding a worldview which includes the nonvisible, the nonmaterial, the spiritual, you keep body, mind and soul in right relationship. I see your morning Tai Chi, hear your drumming and dancing in the quad. I know your songs, your plays, and I read your poems. Most important, many of you cultivate an inward teacher, a voice of wisdom inside yourselves which will be with you the rest of your lives—in loneliness and alienation, in thoughtful encounters with other people, in dialogue with great ideas and works, in love and in emptiness, in hunger and in richness, in solitude and in community.

Now when you look at yourselves in the mirror, I want you to see something of what I see. I want you to see your own strengths and the beauty of the souls, the future, you are making in this universe with no boundaries. You may have no idea who you will be with, where you will live, or what work you will finally choose, but you can know and live your deepest truths. And *that*, after all, is what matters most for now and tomorrow.

Thirty years ago, I was on the edge of a revolution, a transformation, and didn't know it. You, too, are on the edge of a transformation, a new millennium, but you *do know* it. And because you are working to free yourselves from so many intellectual, psychological, and spiritual boundaries, because you are gifted and able and blessed, I trust you will continue to give your lives to connecting, to serving, to creating, to remembering that Tewa Indian prayer: Your life is my life; my life is your life; our lives are one life.

Condoms and Coercion
The Maturity of Self Determination
Edwin J. Delattre

Dean, School of Education, Boston University

Presented to
the Chelsea Management Team and concerned citizens,
Chelsea Public Schools, Chelsea, Massachusetts,
January 14, 1992

This presentation was given in the context of a ten-year partnership, established between Boston University and the Boston Public Schools, to deal jointly with issues facing the local schools. Chelsea Public Schools is one of the school districts in Boston; the Chelsea Management Team is comprised of members from Chelsea schools and Boston University.

Good evening, ladies and gentlemen. I am happy to be with you tonight as we renew our work in behalf of the Chelsea Public Schools, and the broader community, in this new year of 1992.

Much has changed since our last meeting on December 10. You will recall that on November 12, we addressed the question of whether we would distribute free condoms to students through our Health Clinic in Chelsea High School. After twenty-six presentations by members of the public, followed by extensive discussion within the Management Team, a majority of the Management Team members voted against the resolution to do so. We did adopt a companion resolution to provide comprehensive health and sex education in the Chelsea Public Schools.

Shortly after that meeting, the Chelsea School Committee formally requested that we reconsider the question of condom distribution. We addressed the issue once more on December 10.

Again, after hearing the views of many fellow citizens, including students, a majority of us voted against such a policy.

On December 19, the Chelsea School Committee, by a vote of 6 to 0, overruled the Management Team on this question of policy. And so, for a third time, *despite* the gravely pressing educational issues that we are obligated to treat in the interest of Chelsea students and their families, we must turn to the question of condom distribution in the High School—and to the policies within which Chelsea High School will meet the ruling of the School Committee. I hope that soon we will be able to return to the educational matters that constitute the rightful and primary concerns of the Chelsea Schools, and, indeed, of all schools.

In November and December, I spoke in reply to those who expressed the belief that we should distribute condoms in the High School, explaining in summary form why I consider such a policy inimical to the educational mission of the schools. My reasoning clearly did not persuade the advocates of condom distribution at Chelsea High School, in spite of the fact that condoms are already available free of charge at eight sites in the 1.8-square-mile area of Chelsea.

Free condoms are available for distribution from the MGH-Chelsea Health Clinic at 100 Bellingham Street; from ROCA at 184 Washington Avenue; from Choice Thru Education at 160 Pearl Street; from Centro Hispano at 5 Everett Avenue; from the Chelsea Substance Abuse Clinic at 100 Everett Avenue; from Concilio Hispano at 380 Broadway; from Washington Cove Variety Store at 181 Washington Avenue; and from Magic Shears Hair Salon at 136 Washington Avenue. Surely, no one can reasonably suppose that any adolescent in Chelsea would have difficulty getting free condoms if he or she wanted them.

I sought to explain, with consideration for the deeply felt passion of condom distribution advocates, why the distribution of condoms is an affront to the educational opportunities we owe the students in all of Chelsea's schools. I wanted to encourage reflection among students and others on policy matters in general and on what constitutes faithful service to the public, and so I tried to be inviting in my observations.

Even though, in December, the students provided only a role-playing presentation in favor of their preferences, rather than reasoned arguments for a position, I opted for a restrained response. I continue to hope that our students will not come to believe that their own and others' insensitive caricatures of school officials who are devoted to them is an adequate substitute for considered explanation and reasoning. In any case, I sought to stick to the point of the mission of the schools.

I believed then that the educational experience and judgment within the School Committee were sufficient that its members would support our resolution to provide comprehensive health and sex education for students but not the distribution of condoms in the High School. Though I continue to respect the School Committee and their dedication to students, I was clearly mistaken in believing that they would support our position. And so, tonight, faced with a coercive mandate to do what we ought not to do, I intend to speak my mind—plainly and in hope of minimizing adverse consequences of the School Committee's ruling. I will offer an analysis of our situation, a set of recommendations to the Superintendent, and, in conclusion, I will make a request of the School Committee.

We were told in November and December by condom distribution advocates that school distribution of condoms is not a moral issue but rather an issue of life and death. We were told, by the same people, that we have a moral obligation to do everything in our power, at all times, to save lives. The incoherence—indeed, contradiction—between these claims reflects the failure of condom distribution advocates to perceive the fact that *all* life-and-death issues are morally consequential; that questions of what schools have the right and the duty to do in the interest of their students are irreducibly moral questions; and that *how* schools should endorse and sustain the honorable conduct of personal life is a moral issue of the most basic and profound sort.

The plain fact is that if our only moral duty were to save lives—at whatever cost to other ideals of life—on statistical grounds, we would have to raise the legal age for acquiring a driver's license to at least twenty-five; we would have to reduce interstate highway speed limits to 35 mph or less; we would have to force everyone in America to undergo an annual physical examination; we would have to outlaw foods that contribute to bad health; we would have to prohibit the use of tobacco and advertisements for it, and spend huge resources to enforce those laws; we would have to eliminate rights of privacy in the home in order to minimize the possibility of domestic violence; we would have to establish laws to determine who can safely bear children, and therefore who is allowed to become pregnant; we would have to make AIDS and drug testing mandatory for all citizens at regular intervals; we would have to do away with the rights of suspects to due process in order to eliminate open-air drug marketplaces in our cities; we would have to incarcerate, on a permanent basis, all prostitutes who test HIV positive; we would have to announce publicly the name of every person who tests HIV positive in order to safeguard others from possible exposure through sexual activity. And so on.

Saving lives is not the only moral concern of human beings. The prevention of needless suffering among adults, youths, children, infants and unborn babies; the avoidance of self-inflicted heartache; and the creation of opportunities for fulfilling work and for happiness in an environment of safety and justice all merit moral attention as well. And even if saving lives were our only moral concern, there is no reason to believe that distributing condoms in schools is the best way to save lives. Certainly, the distribution of condoms is an unreliable substitute for the creation of a school environment that conveys the unequivocal message that abstinence has greater life-saving power than any piece of latex can have.

Furthermore, even if condoms were the best means of saving lives, there would be no compelling reason for schools rather than parents to distribute condoms; no reason for schools to be implicated in the distribution of condoms when others are willing and eager to do so; no reason for schools to assent to the highly questionable claim that *if* they distribute condoms, they will, in fact, save lives.

We have a duty to make clear to our students in the Chelsea community the implications of sexual involvement with other people who are ignorant of the dangers of sexual transmission of diseases or uncaring about any threat they may pose to the safety of the innocent. Our students need to grasp that if any one of us becomes sexually involved with someone and truly needs a condom or a dental dam because neither we nor the other person knows how much danger of exposure to AIDS that person may be subjecting us to, then we are sleeping with a person who is either staggeringly ignorant of the dangers involved or else is, in principle, willing to kill us. Such a person has not even the decency to wait long enough for informative medical tests to be conducted that would have a chance of disclosing an HIV positive condition; not even the decency to place saving our lives, or anyone else's, above personal gratification. Obviously, if we behave in this way, we, too, are guilty of profound wrongdoing.

This is so inescapably a moral issue—about saving lives—that its omission by condom distribution advocates astounds the imagination. They have said nothing about the kinds of people who are unworthy of romantic love and personal trust, who conceal or ignore the danger they may pose to another's life, even with a condom. These considerations prove yet another fundamental fact of human life: the only things casual about casual sex are its casual indifference to the seriousness of sexual life, its casual dismissal of the need for warranted trust between one individual and another, and its casual disregard and contempt for our personal duty to protect others from harm or death.

We have a duty to explain to students that there is no mystery about discovering and saying what is morally wrong. It is morally wrong to cause needless suffering, and it is morally wrong to be indifferent to the suffering we may cause by our actions. On both counts, sexual promiscuity is conspicuously wrong.

Sexual promiscuity, casual sexual involvement, whether in youth or adulthood, is an affront to all moral seriousness about one's own life and the lives of others. Exposing oneself and others to possible affliction with sexually transmitted diseases is itself morally indefensible, but even where this danger is not present, sexual promiscuity reveals a grave failure of personal character.

A person who is sexually promiscuous inevitably treats other people as mere objects to be *used* for personal gratification, and routinely ignores the possibility of pregnancies that may result in unwanted children whose lot in life will be unfair from the beginning. This is morally wrong; it is an affront to the dignity of human beings, an affront to their right to be treated with concern for their feelings, hopes, and happiness, as well as their safety.

Where promiscuity is shrewdly calculated, it is crudely exploitative and selfish; where promiscuity is impulsive, it is immature and marks a failure of self-control. In either case, promiscuity is incompatible with moral seriousness, because wherever there is promiscuity, there is necessarily an absence of the emotional and spiritual intimacy that anchor genuine love among human beings, love that is healthfully expressed among morally mature people in nonpromiscuous sexual intimacy.

Those who are sexually promiscuous—or want to become promiscuous by successfully persuading others to gratify their desires—routinely seek to exert peer pressure in favor of sexual indulgence, as surely as drug users seek to impose peer pressure in favor of drug and alcohol consumption. Anyone who believes that such persons will not try to overcome resistance to sexual involvement by insisting that the school distributes condoms; that the Health Center says condoms increase your safety, or at least make sex "less dangerous"; that sexual activity is *only* a health issue and not a moral issue, and that condoms eliminate the health problem— anyone so naive ignores entirely, or does not know, the practices of seduction, the manipulativeness among people who treat others as objects to be used for their own pleasure, or the coercive power of adverse peer pressure.

We also have a duty to describe to our students the very real dangers of promiscuity even with condoms. According to research conducted by Planned Parenthood, condoms have a vastly greater rate of failure in preventing pregnancy when used by young unmarried women—36.3 percent—than has been reported by condom distribution advocates. The Family Research Council stresses that this figure is probably low where condom failure may involve possible exposure to AIDS, since the HIV virus is 1/450 the size of a sperm and is less than 1/10 the size of open channels that routinely pass entirely through latex products such as gloves.

The behavior of health professionals with respect to "less dangerous" sex ought to be described to students as well. As reported in the Richmond, Virginia, *Times-Dispatch* ten days ago:

> "Dr. Theresa Crenshaw, a member of the national AIDS Commission and past president of the American Association of Sex Education, Counselors, and Therapists, told a Washington conference of having addressed an international meeting of 800 sexologists: 'Most of them,' she said, 'recommended condoms to their clients and students. I asked them if they had available the partner of their dreams, and knew that person carried the virus, would they have sex, depending on a condom for protection? No one raised their hand. After a long delay, one timid hand surfaced from the back of the room. I told them that it was irresponsible to give advice to others that they would not follow themselves. The point is, putting a mere balloon between a healthy body and a deadly disease is not safe.'" [January 4, 1992, p. A-10]

These reasons of principle and of fact ought to be sufficient to show the hazards of the ruling that has been imposed on us by the School Committee. But there is more to the moral dimension of school distribution of condoms, and those who have claimed otherwise deserve a further account with respect to sexual life itself.

In being forced to distribute condoms in Chelsea High School—to children and adolescents whose emotional and intellectual maturity remain, for the most part, in the balance—we are made to convey to the young the false message that we do not know these things about basic decency, about safety, about the high price of putting everything at risk for instant pleasure. And we are also giving youths whose judgment is still being formed the impression that we do not particularly care about the moral dimensions of sexual life, and that there is no particular reason for them to do so either.

Remember: we have been told here in this room by adults and youths alike that there *is* no moral issue at stake. The acquiescence of the School Committee in condom distribution tacitly affirms that pronouncement. Their message betrays fidelity to high standards of ethics in education and sensitivity to more comprehensive dimensions of respect for justice, self-control, courage, and regard for persons in the articulation of institutional policy and the conduct of personal life.

Those who have told us that we are not faced with a moral issue transparently lack understanding of the fundamentals of moral maturity and character excellence. Their judgment, shallow as it is, betrays the young to a supposed, but implausible, expediency.

We will be told that all this will be covered by conscientious counseling of youths who request condoms. But, despite the best efforts of our well-intentioned health care professionals, it will not be adequately covered—and it will certainly not be covered for the students, and their former classmates who have dropped out of school, who are subject to peer pressure but never seek condoms themselves.

Condom distribution in the schools, even under the most carefully considered conditions, lends itself to the theme we have heard here: that profound dimensions of moral life, including decent treatment of others, have nothing to do with morality. It is not simply that this position is morally incompetent; it is also cruel in its licensing of peer pressure to become sexually active, peer pressure that can be, and often is, selfish, intolerant, even downright vicious.

The School Committee's position has sanctioned such peer pressure and has thereby given approval to forms of behavior and manipulation that cause, among the young, enormous suffering. Condom distribution advocates behave as though they know nothing of human nature and nothing of the unfair pressures to which the young are routinely subjected. The School Committee's decision has now implicated us in teaching the young that we, too, are ignorant of these facts of life as they apply in youth.

The reply of condom distribution advocates to my reasoning is predictable. Sexual activity among the young is inevitable, they will say, even natural, and for reasons of birth control, avoidance of unwanted teenage pregnancies and protection from sexually transmitted diseases, including AIDS, it is better that students should use condoms than not. They will insist that the availability of condoms does not increase the likelihood of sexual activity and that, in any case, many students who use the condoms will be selectively active rather than promiscuous.

The counterarguments are equally straightforward. If we teach the young that sexual activity is what we expect of them, at least some of them will come to expect it of themselves. We have no right to exhibit, or to have, such low expectations—especially toward those whose decisions about whether to become sexually active remain in the balance or who hope to live in an environment where restraint is not only respected but genuinely admired.

And for those who *are* sexually promiscuous—for whatever

motives—whether they act in this way to aggrandize themselves; or to exert power over others; or to gain prestige, or physical pleasure, or peer approval; whether they are sexually active because of a desperate and doomed hope of securing affection and attention; or from failure to grasp alternatives; or from ignorance of consequences of promiscuity; or from a mistaken belief that intercourse and intimacy are the same—for all of them, if it is better that they should use condoms than not, how does it follow that *we* should give them the condoms *in* the High School?

In logic—and in fact—it does *not* follow. Even if it is true that promiscuity with condoms and dental dams is physically less dangerous than promiscuity without them, this ostensible fact in no way suggests or implies that *we* should be in the business of distributing condoms—as surely as the fact that filtered cigarettes are less harmful than unfiltered ones does not imply that we should be distributing free filtered cigarettes in the Chelsea Public Schools. We should instead be standing on the side of peer pressure against casual sex, and we should be providing resolute support for such peer pressure because it is morally right and because it has a distinctive and irreplaceable power to save lives.

Some condom distribution advocates insist that because we now have a health clinic in the High School, we are obliged to defer to the judgment of experts in health care on this subject. They claim that these experts do not try to tell us what we should do as educators, and we should not tell them what to do in matters of health and health-related services.

This artificial and illusory bifurcation of education and health is based on the false premise that what health officials do in the High School contains no educational lessons and teaches nothing about institutional policy or the decent conduct of personal life.

In this particular matter, health experts have clearly attempted to teach the public—including students—that the High School is an appropriate condom distribution site, while dismissing as irrelevant questions of educational mission and duty; and social service agency leaders have advocated that policy by pandering to and proselytizing for the view naively expressed by students that there are no moral issues implicit in the policy. They have exceeded their competence in questions of morals.

Furthermore, it is well understood by all of us that condoms are fallible. We have not adequately addressed problems of potential legal liability for Boston University, the City of Chelsea, the Chelsea Public Schools, and the School Committee. Yet both health professionals and social service personnel have, in our previous meetings, explicitly dismissed as trivial the prospect of legal liability for our institutions, as though they were qualified not only in matters of ethics but also in matters of law. In both respects, they have acted as educators—miseducators.

In doing so, they have potentially undermined the achievement of healthy levels of self-assertion by students, putting that achievement at risk from dangerous peer pressure. They have likewise jeopardized the achievement of self-respect among students by teaching them that even a questionable expediency is more important than mature judgment, personal restraint, and respect for the well-being of other people.

These are the facts of our present situation. We have been brought to a moment when we are no longer able to do what we ought to do in the High School, but are forced to do what is educationally wrong. We have been driven to this condition by a collection of flawed arguments about educational policy, about ethical life, and about law.

The principal questions left to the Management Team now, the questions left to our prerogatives of judgment in this matter, concern the implementation of the condom distribution policy. Accordingly, I propose to the Superintendent of Schools a series of requirements to be met for the distribution of condoms in Chelsea High School. I believe that it is within the authority of the Superintendent of Schools to establish policies concerning the distribution of condoms, and that our primary responsibility tonight is to offer recommendations for his consideration. Therefore, let me recommend several applicable courses of action.

First, we should permit the free distribution only of the most reliable condoms manufactured, whatever their cost to Massachusetts General Hospital.

Second, Massachusetts General Hospital should provide an explicit indemnification to Boston University, the City of Chelsea, and the School Committee from all malpractice or other legal liability.

Third, the High School should send a letter to all parents describing the services offered by the Health Clinic and informing the parents that condoms do not make sex safe.

Fourth, under no circumstances should any teacher or administrator in Chelsea High School be involved in the distribution of condoms.

Fifth, these condoms should be distributed only in conjunction with qualified counseling in their use and qualified instruction in ethics—both to be provided by health personnel in the Clinic. The specific instruction to be given in both domains should be prepared in general form in writing—in English and other languages—for review and approval by the Management Team and by the Superintendent of Schools.

Sixth, the counseling should include instruction about all sexually transmitted diseases and their consequences in suffering, endangerment of future pregnancies, effects on offspring, and possible death. This instruction should include education about all conditions under which AIDS can be transmitted, not only in various forms of intercourse and oral sex, but by transfusions, shared use of contaminated needles, intrusive medical treatments performed by afflicted health care professionals, and other varieties of behavior against which condoms and dental dams afford no protection.

Seventh, students should be given a written examination, and be required to pass it, on these subjects before becoming eligible to receive condoms from the Health Clinic in the High School.

Eighth, no student should ever be excused from classes or study periods to receive such counseling and instruction. Only lunch period or time before and after school should be available for this purpose—in keeping with the educational mission and priorities of the schools.

Ninth, any student who requests condoms, and is not exempt by statute from requirements of parental consent for medical treatment, should be made to bring a signed letter from a parent or guardian expressing approval of distribution of condoms to this daughter or son—and explicitly absolving Boston University, the Chelsea Public Schools, the City of Chelsea, and all of their personnel, from all legal liability for any consequences that may follow—*all* liability. If the parent or guardian cannot, for any reason, provide such a letter, then legally satisfactory approval should be given in person, witnessed and recorded. The form such letters are to take should be reviewed by Boston University legal counsel before the Health Clinic informs the parents and guardians what is required of them. When such a letter is received, it should be confirmed by telephone by a Health Clinic employee and a log kept noting the date and time of the telephone confirmation. If the parent or guardian does not have a telephone, then receipt of the written approval should be confirmed by return mail. All letters and visitation and telephone logs should be kept permanently on file to safeguard the University, the Schools, and the City of Chelsea from future legal actions.

No doubt, critics will reply that such policies for condom distribution will reduce the likelihood that students will seek condoms through the Health Clinic and that the policies are therefore self-defeating. Perhaps they will insist that such policies undermine the capacity of the Health Clinic to save lives.

Their predictions about the attractiveness of the Health Clinic as a condom distribution site may be true. But their claim about the power to save lives is not. If we are to be forced to distribute condoms, then I want us to do so in a way that shows unmistakably our clear understanding of the duties and aspirations, the respect for other people and the effort to make the best possible people of ourselves, that are central to a life well and honorably lived.

I want our students to know that we are unwilling to grant free rein to peer pressure that obstructs their self-interest and jeopardizes their happiness. I want them to understand that we *cannot* save their lives—only they can do that for themselves—and that we work to sustain educational policies that advance their ability to do so, in the short run and in the long run, as they assume progressively greater responsibility for their own destinies.

As much as anything, I am motivated in my observations tonight, and in my proposals of policy, by the vivid, unforgettable memory of the youngest of the students who spoke publicly here on November 21 in favor of condom distribution in the High School. She had not yet reached the age for high school, she told us, and she beseeched us to distribute condoms in the High School because if we did not, the youths slightly older than she, and indeed the children of her own age, would die. The sincerity of her belief was clear in her tone and in her eyes that glistened in these bright lights, filled, I thought, with tears.

I want that child to be told the truth.

I want her to learn that her generation, and those a bit older than she, do not have to die in youth. That many of her peers will not die of sexually transmitted diseases; instead, they will learn to avoid casual sex because it is irreducibly dangerous, and because it diminishes self-respect. That untimely sexual activity is no more inevitable than individual human beings make it, by their own decisions and actions. That there are many safeguards against lethal and destructive diseases, all within the power of the young to bring to bear in their own behalf—and that of these, the most important and trustworthy are not condoms and dental dams. That among these safeguards are a due regard for personal safety; an unwillingness to engage in activities that may later put at risk people you come to love; a rejection of promiscuity as a way of life; the learned ability to choose friends and possible spouses who deserve your trust and your love; the courage to rise above adverse peer pressure; the maturity of self-determination; the acquisition of habits of learning that open the doors of opportunity and dramatically expand the domain of future friendships and loves; and the patience to defer gratification until it is timely, healthy, and warranted.

I want her to know that we understand the downside consequences of our distribution of condoms in the High School, and to know that, all the same, we respect the rules and limits to our authority. Therefore, we are trying to make the best, in good faith, of a bad thing.

I want all of our students in Chelsea to know what is at stake here—and, above all, what lies in their power alone, not ours, to accomplish decisively in the way of saving lives. I want them to know that betting your life—or letting someone else bet your life—on a condom is a gamble that only one in eight hundred experts on sexual behavior is willing to risk, and that if our own students behave otherwise, they make a mockery of their stated commitment, expressed over and over again in this room, to saving lives. And I want all the students who have taken it upon themselves to distribute condoms in Chelsea High School to know that this is the gamble they have invited their classmates to take—and this, in a community where health officials themselves express fear over current levels of AIDS in the population.

Short of all this, we will have been incompetent, and therefore immoral, teachers. Such incompetence on our part would be a disgrace far more shameful than being forced to distribute condoms, and every student, every citizen in Chelsea, deserves to learn that we know it.

Let me conclude, as I promised, with a request of the School Committee. In December, the Committee asked the Management Team to reconsider its position on condom distribution in Chelsea High School, and, in good faith, we did so. I would like now to submit the analysis I have offered tonight to each member of the School Committee, to ask that they read it, and, at their meeting on January 23rd, reconsider supporting our judgment that condoms should not be distributed in the High School. I make this request as a colleague and not an adversary, and in the awareness that Boston University and the School Committee are united by a common dedication to the lives and interests of Chelsea students.

Thank you.

Increasing Productivity on the Farm
Introducing the 722 Grain Cart

Daniel M. Ellerbrock

Student, Ohio State University

Presented to
a presentational speaking class, Ohio State University,
Columbus, Ohio, spring, 1993

In this presentation, Dan Ellerbrock assumed the role of a dealer of farm equipment, introducing a new grain cart at a trade show. The presentation begins when he is approached by a potential customer.

It's nice, isn't it?

Customer: Yeah.

Hi, my name's Dan.

Customer: I'm Nick.

I see you're looking at our front grain cart.

Customer: Yeah, it's great.

You own one of these?

Customer: No, I don't.

About how many acres do you farm?

Customer: About 6,000.

6,000?

Customer: Yeah.

What do you use—about three or four combines for that?

Customer: Four.

Four?

Customer: Yeah.

Well, the unique thing about the grain cart here is that it eliminates one of the four combines. You use this $20,000 grain cart to eliminate a $120,000 combine. You can unload your three other combines on the go, so you never have to stop, which is the biggest downtime in unloading combines. The price of fixing one of these up compared to a combine is smaller than you can imagine.

Customer: Great.

One of the nice characteristics of our grain cart here is our corner-unloading auger. There's a patent on this auger system, which gives much better visibility than the rear- and center-unloading augers.

Customer: It's great.

If you look down here, you see our gear box. This is all just re-done down here—all reinforced with hardier gears and a stronger box. It allows for quicker unloading and less breakdown. If you'll look down here underneath the axle, you'll see that our axles are adjustable, so you can change your spacing to fit your row. And as you can see, it's very strongly built, so it won't fall apart when you're going through all those rock fields.

Customer: Uh-huh.

And on our 772 model here, you have a 750-bushel capacity. It allows you to put all three of your combines into it and then load it onto the truck. The grain truck will also allow you to leave your truck sitting on the road, where you don't have to bring it into the field, whereas if you're unloading your combine, you have to bring it in.

Customer: Right.

This obviously will make you more productive on your end rows. Our unloading auger is also available in the 14 or 17 inch, which allows faster or slower motion—whatever you want. You also have this option over here, which is a scale that allows you to calculate how many bushels are in each cart going in, so you don't have to go back and take all your slips at the end of the day and go to a computer or a calculator and figure it all out.

Customer: Wow.

I have pamphlets over here if you want to come with me and take a look at these. This pamphlet explains our 772 model. It has all the specifications on it. The dual wheels are an option that can also reduce compaction. We have many different sizes to fit your needs. This is the latest thing we've come out with—lightfoot here. It's in place of the track system that you have on tanks and tractors. This is a real nice invention—I really like it. It reduces the pounds per square inch. It will reduce compaction even more than a track system, which is the lightest thing they have now, by at least 25 pounds per square inch, which is a really nice option. We have the prices listed here for the cart we're looking at here—the 772. Without any of the options on it, it's basically a $14,000 cart. If you get the scale option and the lightfoot, that would bring it up to about $22,000—over $100,000 less than a combine would be.

Customer: That's a great deal.

It is. It is a great deal.

Customer: Right.

Do you have any questions about it?

Customer: Does it come in any other colors?

Yes. We have it in green and red to go with your John Deere or your International tractor.

Customer: You always want that to match.

Yes. You've gotta have your cart match your tractor! If you have any questions, feel free to call the toll-free number listed on the pamphlet here. If you're looking into buying one, just give our dealership a call—they're right down the road. That number is also on the pamphlet. They'll be glad to give you more information.

Customer: OK. Thanks a lot.

Thanks for stopping by.

Customer: Thanks very much.

A Flair for Fashion
A Welcome to New Employees

Erika Fair

Student, Ohio State University

Presented to
a presentational speaking class, Ohio State University,
Columbus, Ohio, spring, 1993

*In this presentation, Erika Fair assumed the role of the
owner of Erika Fair's Fashion Fair International,
welcoming new employees to her company.*

Welcome to Erika Fair's Fashion Fair International. I would
personally like to express my congratulations and wishes for good
luck to each of you. As you know, you were hired because of your
flair for fashion and your sense of individuality. This company is
built on employees like you.

As each of you knows, my company has a very individual style.
Our clothes express the feminine side of a woman. These clothes
are playful yet sophisticated, exciting yet subtle, durable yet
delicate. Our clothes say, "I'm a professional, a mother, a wife, and
even an athlete." Our clothes are versatile. For example, with this
belt and these earrings, this outfit says, "Let's go to work, let's give
a speech, or even let's have a romantic dinner." Get rid of the belt,
throw on a pair of flats, and it says, "I'm ready for a day of shopping
or just a day of relaxation."

This is where you come in. You know our reputation, you know
what our clothes say and how to wear them. All you have to do is
help build this reputation. As buyers, you are skilled enough to
know what Erika Fair says and what it doesn't. I expect each of you
to assert your individuality when faced with a buying decision but
at the same time to be mindful of the company's look.

Look around you—these are your team members. You need to know each other. You need to be able to work with each other as a family unit, to be able to trust one another's judgments, and, at the same time, to be able to accept one another's downfalls.

You are at the top of the line, and I already cherish each of you as a part of the family. If you ever have a problem, feel free to contact me, even at home, if necessary. Think of these headquarters as your home away from home and me as your mom away from mom. I'm here not as a disciplinarian but as an advisor, friend, and confidante.

You were hired because you are the best at what you do, and you all are here because you know that Erika Fair Fashions is the best. The best working with and for the best—what more can we ask for?

Again, I would like to express my sincere congratulations and wishes of good luck to each of you, and I hope that your experience here at Erika Fair Fashions International is rewarding and exciting for you.

Meet Your Manager
A Self-Introduction

Erika Fair

Student, Ohio State University

Presented to
a presentational speaking class, Ohio State University,
Columbus, Ohio, spring, 1993

In this presentation, Erika Fair assumed the role of a newly hired fashion manager of a department store, introducing herself to her staff.

Good morning. By now, most of you know who I am. My name is Erika Fair, and I've been hired as your new fashion manager. I'd like to tell you a little bit about myself, where I've been, and what I plan to do in this store.

I'm 25 years old, and I'm from Columbus, Ohio. I received my bachelor's degree in fashion design and retail from Ohio State, and I minored in business. I've had a wide variety of jobs and have been in this business since I was 18 years old. During college, I interned at the May Company for two years. There I was able to shadow a fashion manager to see what he did, and I did floor retail like most of you do here. Later, I moved to the Lazarus store in Columbus, and I worked on floor retail, helping customers. After I graduated from college, I moved to Marshall Field's in City Center in Columbus as a fashion coordinator. There I was able to help the department store achieve a smaller look, using different types of displays and lights and working with the clothing worn by the sales staff.

My most recent position has been at The Limited in Columbus. There, I helped the store change its color scheme. As many of you know, The Limited used to put its jeans on the right and its shorts on the left and its dressy clothes in the back. But we changed it to all the reds and corals in the front—or whatever the color of the year was—to make the store look more inviting. We put the darker colors in the back. We also helped utilize the small space of the store by changing the displays.

Basically, I'm here to help do the same thing in our store—set up displays, make the windows look inviting, help the employees develop an even better look. In helping the employees develop a better look, I'm going to ask you to dress alike. This doesn't mean we'll all wear the same things or you'll have to wear the store clothes. What I have in mind is that we'll all be casual on Mondays, for example, and if we decide to be dressier on Tuesdays, we'll all be dressier on Tuesdays. That way, some of us aren't in jeans and T-shirts and some in dresses.

In the windows, to make them more inviting, I plan to devote one of each of the windows to the different departments in the store—one for women's fashions, one for juniors', children's, men's, and so on so that anybody who walks past the store will see something in which they might be interested.

I want to have fun here, and I hope we'll all enjoy ourselves while we're doing business. If we all work together, we'll be able to improve the look of our store and enhance the satisfaction of our customers.

I'm looking forward to working with all of you.

The Coming Chill

Sally Miller Gearhart

Professor Emeritus, Speech and Communication Studies,
San Francisco State University

Presented at
a candlelight march and rally in Civic Center Plaza,
San Francisco, California, November 27, 1988

This presentation was given at a march commemorating the tenth anniversary of the deaths of Harvey Milk, member of the Board of Supervisors, and George Moscone, mayor of San Francisco. They were killed by Dan White, another member of the Board of Supervisors, who was angered by Moscone's refusal to reappoint him to the Board of Supervisors. Shortly before the presentation was given, George Bush had been elected President; he had condemned liberalism and, in particular, the American Civil Liberties Union during the campaign.

Hello, Harvey, wherever you are.

It's the end of another Thanksgiving weekend in your city and, as you can see, we're all standing here in the glow of candles—thousands of intrepid warriors, your friends, remembering you and George tonight, whether we knew you in life or only in the spirit you left behind.

We're trying to find the hope in our hearts that you told us we must have. It is not easy.

Don't mistake me. There are bright spots:

Art Agnos is our mayor.

Harry has been filling the Board of Supervisors with compassion and integrity every time it's threatened to slip back into easy answers or mediocrity or just plain sleaze. He's the head of the Board now as well as its heart.

> Cleve Jones and thousands who have turned seamstress and
> stevedore are wrapping the world in—would you believe?—a
> quilt of healing.
>
> Moved by your spirit, all of us lesbians and gay men and
> bisexuals have been coming out everywhere we can, on
> busses and in supermarkets and in the laundromats of the
> nation.

But that hope you insisted upon has gotten more and more
elusive in this decade, Harvey. Or else it seems buried by our
despair. Or frozen into immobility by a conservative wind that
sweeps colder and colder these days across the nation and over your
city.

Since you left us the ranks of your friends and our community
have been decimated by an epidemic. We can't get money for care
or humane research because we have to pay for a Starwars Defense
System and the destruction of Central America.

And we're about to homeport a nuclear battleship whose
military personnel will change the very face of the city you loved
so much. With the Missouri here we will introduce into the Bay Area
such a heavy reactionary political element that we may lose forever
our identity as the stronghold of California's progressive politics,
as its soul of individual freedom. And with the loss of the Bay Area,
the state of California may well fall to the growing chill of that
conservative wind. I believe that this is part of the deliberate and
long-range agenda of the political Right.

In our more optimistic moods we console ourselves with the
fact that increased militarization means at least that we may die
fast because the Missouri guarantees our top priority as a target for
the nuclear warheads that have more than doubled in number since
you left us.

The flag of the United States, which most of us grew up
respecting, is now the flag most universally despised by the world's
poor and hungry people.

With the march of that flag over more and more of the globe,
Mother Earth is reeling. We kill two species per day of her animal
and plant life.

Even her trees here in Civic Center Plaza are to be cut down
because they give shelter to the growing thousands of San
Francisco's homeless people. And, as the *Chronicle* noted, a treeless
plaza will make easier the control of large demonstrations. Like this
one.

The hole in the earth's ozone is the size of continental United
States and we're still pumping out the chloro-fluoro-carbons that
will make it bigger.

The three greatest tools of the century—the electronic media, the computer industry, and biomedical technology with its genetic engineering—are overwhelmingly in the hands of the rich and the greedy, the enemies of humanity, the enemies of the earth.

It's hard to find hope against all this, Harvey, particularly when instead of Jesse Jackson there's a person entering the White House who threatens to leave it four or eight years from now with the whole of Central America under his thumb and the Bill of Rights in tatters at his feet.

He has beside him a very dangerous and like-minded young man who would not hesitate to suspend indefinitely not only crucial social service programs but the very civil liberties that this nation is built on, all in the name of his understanding of law and order and god.

These two men legitimize exactly the kind of violence that took you and George away from us ten years ago.

And though we keep each other buoyed up with hearty words and testimonies of tiny victories, we still shiver in deep nights of restlessness as we think of even simply the most immediate tasks confronting us:

> the task of holding back the spill of more Central American blood, and more South African and Semitic blood, and the blood of billions more non-human animals;
>
> the task of stalling and maneuvering to keep abortion rights in existence;
>
> the exhaustion of watchdogging every piece of legislation and every arrest so that we can guard the freedom of our press to publish a full range of ideas and cultural expressions, so that we guard our diversity of religious belief, our right to assemble in gatherings like this one, and our freedom to speak as I speak now—so that we guard these freedoms from the decisions of nine men (and, alas, women) in black robes who stand at the pinnacle of what has begun to pass for justice in this once-great country. Even more than in the last eight years, the task is now to protect the Constitution of the United States from the President of the United States.

The pendulum's inexorable swing toward reactionary politics sweeps before it not only the tropical forest and the carefully woven tapestry of our human rights, not only the individuality of a thousand global cultures, but it sweeps before it as well the stuff of all our dreams—our dreams of health, harmony, love, and life in all its diversity.

Harvey, when you were with us our job was to push the

nation's leaders toward justice, peace, and freedom. Our job was
to move the pendulum to the left. Our job now is to halt—or at least
to hold back—its momentum as it swings to the right. Our job is
to cling to that pendulum and with the sheer weight of our bodies
to stop its upward and final swing toward the monolith, toward the
frozen purity of one value system, one doctrine, one god, one creed,
and one greed.

We aren't in the business of moving forward anymore, Harvey.
We're just in the business of dragging our feet.

And though we hesitate to articulate it—because we want to
think positive thoughts—there is nevertheless abroad among us the
fear, even the conviction, that this time in human history the
pendulum will not return.

The cold chill moves across our liberal bones and bids us say
goodbye to all that has been meaningful to us as responsible citizens
of the earth, of this once-worthy nation, of this City by the Sea.

For, it seems, in the image of William Butler Yeats, some great
beast, its hour come round at last, now slouches toward
Bethlehem—or toward Washington, D.C.—to be born.

But let me assure you, Harvey, that all this does not mean
we're quitting. It only means we have to remember you more often,
you and George,

> that while we have life and breath we will not let San
> Francisco, our City by the Sea, become just another Navy
> town, just another San Diego,
>
> that to the extent that our love and our energy endure, we
> will not give over to the winds of conservatism either our
> city or our state,
>
> that instead, we will daily remind the people of California
> of the values that San Franciscans hold most dear: freedom,
> dignity, diversity, peace, and justice.

On the model that you have given us, Harvey, we will come
out, not only as lesbians and gay men and bisexuals, but we will
come out—yes, Mr. President-Elect—as liberals:

> we will tell our immediate families how priceless are the gifts
> of liberty, we will tell our relatives of that pricelessness, we
> will tell our friends, if indeed they are our friends, we will
> tell our neighbors and the people we work with, the people
> in the stores we shop at. We will tell them all.

We will greet the Bush Administration as card-carrying
liberals, to tell the world that in spite of the decay in Washington,
D.C., the Bill of Rights lives, and that U.S. imperialism stops here

at this peninsula. Right here, at this City by the Sea. Right here, between the bay and the breakers!

And in the meantime, Harvey, when we are resting from fighting, from dragging our feet:

> We will stay alert.
>
> We will conserve our energy.
>
> And breathe.
>
> Dream.
>
> Sing.
>
> Hope.
>
> Send a box of pencils to Nicaragua.
>
> Notice the pigeons in the Safeway parking lot.
>
> Place a flower on George Moscone's grave.
>
> And most of all, Harvey, as again you have taught us to do, we will put our arms around each other
>
> and walk side-by-side,
>
> remembering you,
>
> loving each other.

Whose Woods These Are

Sally Miller Gearhart

Professor Emeritus, Speech and Communication Studies,
San Francisco State University

Presented to
the Western Speech Communication Association Convention,
Portland, Oregon, February 18, 1980

This presentation was a response to papers presented on the program, "Narrative as Communication." It was partly inspired by "It Was a Dark and Stormy Night; or, Why Are We Huddling About the Campfire?" by Ursula K. Le Guin.

The big stand-off was about to be over. The showdown was here. The heads of three world powers each held a thumb over a doomsday button. They had tried everything. And everything hadn't worked. Now, no one of them willing to give an inch, they prepared to send the planet into its total annihilation. The only question was, which of them would have the satisfaction of being the last to die.

Suddenly one of them, Thomas Ivanovitch Woo by name but Ivan for short, remembered a promise that in a weak moment he had made to his wife. "Wait a minute, fellows," he said. "Before we do this number we might as well give the women a chance. We got nothing to lose." The others agreed.

So Ivan called his wife and asked her how to get in touch with this Great Mother she was always talking about. His wife gave him three instructions: "Shut up. Go into the woods. And listen."

So Ivan shut up, went into the only forest left on the planet and stood and listened. Pretty soon he sensed some sort of presence and he asked an old, old question: "What must we do?"

The answer was prompt and fairly direct: "Disarm."

Since that was clear enough Ivan went back to his colleagues and told them what the Great Mother had said. And they all disarmed their nations, right down to the last bullet. Ivan went back to the woods and asked the same question again. This time the answer was equally prompt: "Decentralize."

And so the world decentralized its population, its business and government. Time and again Ivan went back to the woods and time and again the Great Mother directed him in the re-making of the world. He did not even argue with some things that seemed of a strictly personal concern to her like the requirement that women be given all the say-so about sex and reproduction, and the requirement that all future planning hold the male population to twenty percent, or that the whole world acknowledge the primacy of the female of the species and embrace the values of nonviolence, nurturance, and cooperation.

"Yeah, yeah, yeah," said Ivan, pretty tired of it all by this time. Off he went and saw to it that all these things were accomplished.

One day when he came back to the Great Mother he was pretty smug. "Say, G.M.," he began. "It's really working. There's a pretty good world out there. Thanks a lot." And he started to go.

"Just a minute."

Ivan turned back.

"You haven't even started yet."

"Whaddya mean?"

"I've had to be pretty directive up to this point. But I won't do that much longer. It's time now for you to begin cleaning up your communication."

"My what?"

"Shut up. Go deeper into the woods. Listen harder."

So Ivan went deeper into the woods and tried to listen harder. He sat for many days in the forest trying to listen. It was not at all easy. Finally a big oak tree said to him: "Hello." Ivan was so relieved that he sprang up and hugged the tree, an action pleasing to the tree since in all its experience the one thing that men do not do to trees is hug them, much less with tears running down their cheeks.

When he sat down again Ivan remembered that his mission was communication, so he tried to decide on his general purpose. Should he entertain, inform or persuade the tree? Since he had been in politics all his life he naturally decided on the persuasive mode. "Tree," he began, moving straight to his proposition, "you must help me and the rest of mankind with our communication problem."

In response the tree cried out in pain and shrank away from him. Clearly he had done the wrong thing. "What is it, what is it? What did I do?"

"Too violent," wailed the tree. "You're trying to change me, and that hurts."

"By asking you to help me?"

"You didn't ask. You didn't even say you wanted or needed something. You told me what I must do."

"Oh," said Ivan. This was going to be difficult. He sat for a while and finally it dawned on him—if he simply opened up, said only what he wanted or needed, and was himself willing to change, then maybe he and the tree could change together. Ivan was ecstatic at this idea, and having been through EST training he was undaunted and eager to try again.

"Well, tree," he said. "I won't persuade. I'll inform you. I want to tell you something. About . . . about trees. Trees. Trees are a type of vegetation found. . . ."

Again the tree reacted, somewhat more mildly this time but enough to let him know that he was still behaving violently. "You're still trying to do something to me," said the tree. "You might just as well put a chain saw to my throat. Instead of trying to inform me you could. . . ."

"I could . . . ?" prompted Ivan.

The tree was silent.

"I could . . . ?"

"Do just what you're trying to do now?" suggested the tree.

Ivan exploded. "What I'm trying to do now? What I'm trying to do now is find out something." He stopped abruptly.

The tree seemed to smile.

And then Ivan was truly in despair. "What can I do," he said to himself. "What is there left? If I can't persuade but can only be open to change, if I can't instruct but must only discover, what can be the nature of my discourse with others?" Truly a puzzle.

He sat for many hours, thinking and listening, thinking to himself, listening to the trees, the grass, the small animals. Finally he said to the tree, "Tree, I've been sitting here for hours puzzling over this thing. First I tried reasoning it out but that didn't work. Then I tried getting in the mood of being all vulnerable and open, not trying to persuade you at all but being willing to change with you. But still nothing happened. Then I tried getting in the mood of just plain learning from you or with you but that didn't work either. Now here I sit, dog tired, and still not able to communicate with you without hurting you."

"Well, you just did it," said the tree.

"???????" said Ivan.

"You just told me a story. About what you've been going through in your head. It was in chronological order. That's the best beginning you've made."

"A story?" Then again Ivan was blessed with illumination. "Yeah! Yeah! You mean I entertained you! That's it! The only nonviolent way to communicate is to entertain! Telling stories— that's what the Toastmaster Club said all along!" He jumped up in exuberance and in sheer release of tension he began to do a buck-and-wing for the tree. "Let me entertain you," Ivan sang.

Again the tree shrank back as if offended.

Ivan stopped abruptly, mid-kick, his face a mask of astonishment. "I'm still trying to do something *to* you right?" he said to the tree. "*To you,* and not *for us.*"

"Right."

Ivan collapsed again to his thinking/listening position. So even stories could hurt if they tried to change people or things. There must be a difference, he mused, between wanting things to change and wanting to change things. The moment he thought that, a good feeling washed over him. Then instead of entertaining the tree he could simply express himself. And then if the tree expressed itself. . . .

He tried it. "Tree, I want to tell a story." And he picked the first fairy tale that occurred to him, one that he barely remembered. But as he warmed to his task of the telling, he found that the words he was uttering themselves generated other words. Soon he began remembering easily and soon there were brand new images, new ideas and feelings that flew by so fast within him that he had trouble getting them out. He paid less and less attention to what he wanted the tree to think of him, even though he was of course still very much aware of the tree's presence, and more and more attention to the story he was telling. He began to enjoy the telling and when he had finished he was sure he heard sighs of appreciation and excitement.

To his amazement another tree in the forest spoke up. "I have a story too," it said. And when it had finished its story there was another tree and another story, another squirrel and another story. Ivan felt himself to be inside a great matrix, a womb, where he and the entire forest shared a constantly changing and intensely intimate reality.

Deep into the night trees and animals told stories of their past, of the things they had observed, of the things they had heard about. They told stories of the future, how they feared it might be, how they hoped it would be.

It was dawn when Ivan rose to his feet to start back to the world of politics. He knew now at least one way that they might begin. Good reason in controversy would have to wait a while. And so would that old taskmaster, justification. He had a story to tell. And he suspected his colleagues had some too.

When he pulled up his chair at the World Council and the whole assembly drew their attention to him, an old enemy-turned-friend said, "Well Ivan, what have you got for us this time?" The whole assembly laughed heartily. Ivan smiled.

"Shut up," he said. "Let's go to the woods. And Listen."

A Successful Open House

Karen Goodman

Student, Ohio State University

Presented to
a presentational speaking class, Ohio State University,
Columbus, Ohio, spring, 1993

*In this presentation, Karen Goodman assumed the role
of a real-estate agent for HER Realty. She was about to
hold an open house and was acquainting the seller with
the process involved.*

Well, Michelle, are you ready for your first open house? I know
you've never done this before, so I'm going to go over all the
procedures with you, and we'll get your open house started in about
an hour or so.

First, I want to let you know what we've done to create a
market for your home. This morning, in the Sunday paper, there's
an ad that says, "Open House, 1:00 to 3:00," and it lists a few
qualities of your home. We will get it laminated for you to keep for
your records; I'll have that for you within three or four days. In
addition, this morning, at 9:00 on channel six, the home gallery
for HER real estate featured your home. We sent out mailers to the
entire neighborhood so that all of your neighbors will be invited to
come. Neighbors often know friends who are looking to move or,
sometimes, neighbors just want to move from one house to another.
So that's how we've advertised your home, and we hope to get
positive responses as a result.

The first thing I want you to know is that I'm here to sell your
house. I'm not here to sell myself, I'm not here to sell HER, I'm here
to get your house sold. If a client comes in, my attention will be
on selling your house. But I do want you to understand that, in order

to do that, I will rely on my reputation to help me get them as a client. So I might mention HER or my sales record or my qualities. You'll also notice that information I put out about your house has my picture and the qualifications of HER on it. This is a way to let the client know who and what will be backing the transaction.

Every single person who comes through that door is considered a prospective buyer, and I will treat everyone as a prospective buyer. Every person will sign an open-house book with their address and their phone number, so that I can follow up and get their feedback on your home. For example, every single person might say, "I would have bought the house except that the tile in the living room is really horrendous, and if you would change that, I would seriously consider buying the house." These kinds of comments give us an idea of what people like or dislike about the home and what you might want to change before we have our next open house or before we have our next publication come out about it, if it even goes that far. Hopefully, we'll have it sold much before that even happens. The people who sign that book probably will be a lot of your neighbors, but we still get their names and we still follow up to see what they thought about your house.

Now, I want to go over the actual house. First, as I showed you last week, the fact sheets, which are in the living room, list all of the features of your house and all of the room dimensions. On the front is the picture of your house—that way, if someone is going to six or seven houses today, they know which one is your house and which one to remember that they want to buy. We have several pens on the table, so they can take notes about the house. You might find these lying around the house at the end of the open house today.

After this, together, we'll go through the house, room by room, making sure you haven't made any changes since the last time I was here. We need to make sure that every room is in perfect order, which I discussed with you before, because when people come through, we want them to see the true beauty of your home. Also, to give the house a really bright quality, I'll ask you to turn on as many lights as possible to make the rooms very bright and cheery. I'll ask you to open all the draperies. If you have no objection, because it's a beautiful day, we'll open the front door to let the fresh air come in and give the house a fresh, open feeling.

Do you have any questions about the process or what I've just gone over?

Seller: Yes, I do. What's the reason that you would prefer we leave the house during the open house?

That's a great question. I'm sorry I forgot to address that. When you're going through the process of contracts, it's not fair to you to know who the buyer is. Sometimes, this knowledge can hinder a sale, which you don't want to do and I don't want to do. In case one of your neighbors wants to put a bid on the house, for example, they may want confidentiality, not wanting you to know they want to move. The confidentiality is also for protection for you—it's not necessary for people who come to the open house to know who lives in the home they're looking at.

Seller: Do you want us to turn the answering machine on?

No, please don't turn the answering machine on. Just leave the phone as it is. We listed your phone number at my office. That way, if anyone has any questions about how to get here or whatever, my office can reach me here, and I can give them directions. Anything else?

Seller: I don't think so.

Well, great. I think things are going to run very smoothly today. The open house will be from 1:00 to 3:00. Give me a few minutes after 3:00 to collect everything, and then come back, and I'll let you know how it went.

Exhibiting With Pride

Janet K. Hughes

Artist

Presented at
the University of Missouri, Columbia, Missouri, March 5, 1993

*This presentation was given as part of a panel
discussion of artists whose work had been selected for
inclusion in the Missouri Visual Artists' Biennial. The
artists were asked to discuss their work prior to the
opening of the exhibition.*

She's an exhibitionist
She exhibits with pride
She exhibits her work in the Missouri Visual Artists' Biennial.

She collected her thoughts
    dust
    and her award.

She means what she says
She means well
She now has the means to continue and expand her work.

For her it was a time of renewal
She renewed her spirit
    an old acquaintance
    and her contract at Indiana State University.

She moved from private to public
And enjoyed the exposure.
The exposure was wide.
She exposed herself.
She was well read.

She became widely read.
She painted the town
    the picture
    and her lips.
Her lips were read.
Her lips were red.

She moved from the margin
Into the center
And preferred the view.

It's Been a Quiet Week in Lake Wobegon

Garrison Keillor

Humorist

Presented on
"A Prairie Home Companion,"
St. Paul, Minnesota, September 5, 1987

This presentation was Garrison Keillor's monologue on his weekly radio program, "A Prairie Home Companion," in which he discusses the news of Lake Wobegon, an imaginary town in Minnesota.

Well, that song just leads me right into talking about Lake Wobegon. I love you, and I'll show it in a thousand ways. Though it's hard for me to show it. It's hard for me to show it to them because I don't live there anymore. And it's hard for me to show it to you because Lake Wobegon is just a hard town to show. If somebody from Los Angeles came to Lake Wobegon and said, "All right, show us the sights," I'd have to stop and think a minute. Well, let me see, we go down to the Chatterbox, see a bunch of guys in feed caps sitting around drinking coffee. Show you the statue of the unknown Norwegian. Take you up to Our Lady of Perpetual Responsibility Church and have you meet Father Emil. Bet you haven't met anybody just like him before. But otherwise, I'm not sure.

It's kind of a quiet time of year there right now. Until the Fourth of July comes up and Toast and Jelly Days in July, I can't think of any big celebrations. They used to celebrate Flag Day. Now Flag Day's coming up this next week, and they will show flags. The Chamber of Commerce sells 'em. They put 'em in front of all the shops, and everybody hangs a flag in front of their house, usually in front of their porch, but there's not a whole lot to do on Flag Day other than just show the flag, I guess. It's kind of a Lake Wobegon type holiday.

There was a Flag Day celebration—I think it was back in about 1958—when Yalmer Inkvist organized a living flag. They got 400 people to wear red, white, and blue caps and then lined 'em up standing in Main Street in the form of a flag, which I think probably the idea came from a traveling cap salesman because once they were all lined up there, and you know they had stars and the bars and everything, there were not many people left over to appreciate it. A couple of guys up there on the roof of the Central Building, and they said, "Boy, that looks great!" But there were just a couple.

Then somebody got out from the living flag who had a red cap on (he was part of a stripe), and he ran up to the top of the Central Building 'cause he wanted to see it. And then, of course, everybody had to do it. Then everybody had to see the flag. Yalmer says, "Well, let's go in groups," but then if you go in groups that destroys the very thing you're lookin' at, don't it? So one by one, into the Central Building, climb four flights of stairs, go out and lean over the parapet, look down, there's the flag. All right, now it's your turn, Carl. Then Carl came up. Finally, the living flag became kind of a sitting flag. Until finally they got down to the last person. They had been there for hours. They didn't care to hear anything about Flag Day for a long time. Mrs. Olson was the last one. She had a white cap on—she was part of a star. They said, "All right, it's your turn. Go!" She said, "Oh, no, that's all right, I don't need to." They said, "Go! Get up there!" She said, "That's all right, I don't need to; I've seen flags before." I tell you, the whole lower right-hand corner of that flag just grabbed onto her, and they marched her up and they made her look at it. And then they all came back down again. Then somebody wanted to go home and get a camera. They've never done that since. Yes, that's the town where the Fourth of July parade takes four turns around the block there in the middle of town so that participants can drop out and watch it as it goes by and other people get in.

But that's not goin' on this year. And otherwise, I don't know what I would show you. It's kinda quiet there. The gardens are coming along. People like to sit in their backyards and watch sets of onions come up. Great big gardens in that town out behind almost every house.

The porches, the porches are open, everybody's on their porch in the evening. That's nice. They don't believe in air conditioning in Lake Wobegon; they believe it's a sign of ill health. And also a sign of extravagance and corruption and decadence such as brought down the Roman Empire. Roman Empire had air conditioners, you know, and that's why they didn't hear the Barbarians coming was because the windows were all closed. We don't have it in Lake Wobegon. They keep their windows open, and they sit out on their front porches behind the screens, and they sit there with the nectar and the cookies. The front sidewalk is maybe twenty feet away. The front yards aren't big in Lake Wobegon. They save the space for the garden in the back. And people go by on the street. And the people in the porch, there's a whole little ritual about it. People in the porch call out and they say, "Hello, how ya doin'? Beautiful day, isn't it?" And then if they want to, they say, "Why don't ya come on in and sit with us for a bit?" The person on the sidewalk is supposed to say "no" the first time. They say, "No. No, thanks, we're just goin' up the street." It's the second invitation which is the real invitation. "Now, come on in, come on in, sit down." "Well, all right, just for a minute." Walk in, have some nectar and some cookies. Fall asleep. Good place for naps. Front porch. Nobody's offended if you doze off; it's quite common. Good sleeping weather in Lake Wobegon.

I think, though, about the Lundberg family when I think about sleeping. They are a family that sleeps during the day and is kinda restless during the night. They're all big, stocky, phlegmatic Norwegians, your Lundberg family. Very quiet. Sometimes, you'll see 'em sitting on the bench in front of the Chatterbox, kinda swaying, their eyes shut. They're quite peaceful during the day.

It's at night when they really come to. They go up to bed, the Lundbergs do, Carl and Betty, the three boys, all big lunkers, and after a while, about midnight or so, if you're still up, you can hear loud cries coming from the Lundberg home as they're yelling out in their sleep. Not from Betty, now; she's an Olson. And the Olsons were always very sedate sleepers. You kinda have an idea about the Olsons that they would lie down and straighten the covers and fold their hands and put 'em on their bellies and awake eight hours later in the same position.

But Carl is a Lundberg, and how she can sleep in the same bed with him for twenty years, I don't know. Because Carl gets to, he's drowning in his sleep. And he's struggling in the water and swimming, and he's calling out, waving to search planes overhead, dreaming terrible dreams, and ever so often during this warm weather when there's a full moon, you'll have Lundbergs coming out of their homes, sleepwalking, out into town, great big sleeping Lundbergs, moving out from their homes, like some horror movie. Move along, sometimes humming to themselves. Usually a hymn like "Rock of ages, abide with me, fast falls the eventide." You might hear 'em back in your garden, thrashing around back there, picking grass out by big clumps, walkin' around on your tomato plants. And in a town like Lake Wobegon, where nobody locks their front door and nobody even remembers where the key is [much laughing from the audience], I got some Lundberg relatives up there. They remember that branch of the family, yes. You hear some crashing downstairs, that's a Lundberg down there.

Walkin' down the street, sometimes people think like they otta awaken 'em, but it's dangerous to awaken a sleeping Lundberg. You grab one, you know, and you shake 'em and you say, "Ralph, wake up, it's three o'clock in the morning; you're downtown in your shorts." Ralph is likely to wake up and say, "Well, I'm goin' home if you just let go of me." It can be violent. I don't know what causes it; I don't think anyone in Lake Wobegon wants to know. It's some kind of deep-seated frustration, some unhappiness that they can't talk about during the day. They can only wander around like ghosts at night. . . .

That's the news from Lake Wobegon, Minnesota, where all the women are strong and all the men are good looking and all the children are above average.

The Second Report of the Shipwrecked Foreigner to the Kadanh of Derb

Ursula K. Le Guin

Author

Presented to
the Women, Power, and Leadership Conference, sponsored by the
Seattle branch of Antioch University, Seattle, Washington, November, 1984

Your Highness:

I have been trying to tell you a story about a Representative Person of Earth, so that you might be amused by the tale while learning from it, or from the spaces between the words, something about my world, or yours. The trouble is, I have not been able to think of a Representative Person.

I met a member of the House of Representatives once. He was an odd person, not representative at all. He entered the room when the party had been going on for an hour or so, and from the way the host and hostess and others went to him like bits of iron to a magnet, and from the way he spoke in rich tones, it was evident that he was important. Unfortunately I lived in the wrong district and had never heard his name, and so when we were introduced I was puzzled by the curiously professional way he shook my hand, as if handshaking were a profession, and by the way he used his eyes. He used them as a means of looking straight into my eyes with an expression of intense sincerity. I had the impression that he did not see me. I don't know who, or what, he did see. He talked well and loudly, told two fairly dirty jokes at dinner, and laughed. He impinged upon all of us, while none of us seemed to affect him in any way. He exuded himself, while absorbing nothing. From what inexhaustible source, since he never replenished it by drawing upon the rest of the universe, did he draw so much self to exude? When I found out (on the way home) that he was a Representative, I thought that that explained it: his inexhaustible source was power—power itself. He was, as it were, plugged into the main. But this disqualified him as a Representative *Person*. Most people have to generate their own power.

Once upon a time a baby was born and named Soru. When she was little her mother carried her into the fields and laid her in the shade at the field's edge while the work went on. When Soru got bigger she ran about in the village with the other little children, and played down by the stream. The children made boats out of big leaves; Soru liked to make little mud figures of people and set them in the boats. The boats always sank, and the mud figures dissolved quickly in the muddy water, becoming swirls of tiny particles drifting downstream. Soru learned how to prepare food with her mother and aunt and elder sister. With other girls she learned other necessary skills such as sewing, mat-making, roof repair, dancing, fire-tending, milking, storytelling, genealogy, and all the labors of the fields. She was healthy, merry, and industrious, and not long after she attained puberty Anfe's family came to ask about her dowry; presently she became Anfe's wife and went to live in that household. There she worked very hard, but Anfe's three younger sisters were jolly and affectionate, and the four of them were always laughing and playing and joking. Soru's first baby was born on the day it rained after the long drought; the rain beat like great drums, and the child was a beautiful and healthy girl. The next year she had a boy, and the year after that a girl. Anfe's father died then, and the man from Monoy came and insisted that the debt be paid. The family could not pay it all, and he would not accept part payment, so they lost the land. Soru and Anfe and the three babies and Anfe's youngest sister had to move in with Anfe's mother's sister, who was a mean, lazy old woman. That house was so dirty it could not be cleaned, and far too small for them all, but Soru managed. She worked for Tima in the fields. When the chance for a good marriage for Anfe's youngest sister came up, Soru saw to it that a dowry was provided, though she missed her sister-in-law's company, and now while she was in the fields she had to leave the children in the care of the old woman. Anfe was a good-natured man and a hard worker, but he hated being tied down to one job for long; he quit work so often that he couldn't always find it, and went without work sometimes for weeks and months. At such times he would hang around with other men and drink, and come home drunk and treacherous and full of rage; then he and the old woman would quarrel, and the children would hide from them until Soru came home from the fields. One day in the long rains Anfe and the old woman began quarreling again. He began swearing and hitting her. The eldest girl knew that after her father left, the old woman would beat the children, so she took the two little ones and ran to hide down by the river where they often played. The river was swollen with rain and the banks were caving in. The bank fell away under the eldest girl's feet and she was swept away by the river. The little ones came crying to the house. When people came to the field where Soru was working and told her, she sat down on the wet ground and rocked her body, crying out, "Oh, oh, my child of the rain, my child of the rain!" She was five months pregnant then. After that happened, Anfe drove the old woman out of her own house, and she went to live with her granddaughter in Monoy. Anfe got a job he liked, working on the dam they were building upriver; he could only come home twice a month, but he got very good pay. Soru was not well and had to stop working in the fields. She got the house as clean as it could be got, and was content looking after the two children, but she still did not feel well. More than a month before her time she began to bleed, and they could not stop the bleeding; and so she died, and the baby was stillborn. Anfe's elder sister took the two children. Soru lived twenty years, eight months, and four days.

What I don't know how to do, you see, is put Soru and the member of the House of Representatives together so that they make any sense. Soru seems to say, "Work, laugh, grieve, die," and the Representative says, "I, I, I, I," and neither can hear the other. If you put the two together, it does make sentences: I work, I laugh, I grieve, I die. But these sentences mean such different things to Soru and to the Representative! He might even deny that the last two sentences—I grieve, I die—were true. Soru would deny none of them, but she probably would have seen little sense in talking about such things; she went ahead and did them. And maybe sang about them. The Representative also indubitably has worked and laughed and will die, but he does not want these matters mentioned, preferring such terms as "profit incentive," "recreation," "life expectancy." I can't think how he would refer to grief at all— perhaps as "mental health problems." But since Soru simply did not exist, was a total blank, in respect to profit incentive, recreation, life expectancy, and mental health problems, the Representative would be unable to comprehend the fact that she existed, or indeed that anyone else exists; so we are back to his "I, I, I, I." And to the subject of power.

Power is said to be the most important thing on earth. It is said that if Soru had had power—various sorts of power, but all deriving from the sort of power the Representative has—if Soru had been plugged into the main, her life would have been three or four times longer and happier.

The life expectancy of the Representative is certainly more than three times longer than Soru's life and ten times longer than Soru's eldest daughter's life. Is a life expectancy, however, a life? At eleven years old, Soru was a very good dancer. Can people who are plugged into the main dance? Or can they only twitch as the electricity courses through their veins? They say the victims of electrocution and the subjects of electroshock therapy, when the power is switched on, do a sort of dance.

I have a notion that the word "power" has become a form empty of content, which has meaning only as the individual fills it, pours the molten bronze of a life and self into that empty mold. Other such words are "God," "Country," justice," "rights." They are words frequently used by the Representative. But has he ever filled them with anything? Is "I, I, I, I" what should fill those great empty forms?

The architect gives me the blueprint. "There," he says, "there's your house!"

"Very nice! When will you start work on it?"

"Start work? I'm an architect, not a carpenter. It's finished— I've done my work! Why don't you move in?"

So I move into the blueprint. I become very clever at cooking nutritious paper stew, which my family eats all grouped cheerily together in the Dining Area of the blueprint. We furnish the living room with cutouts from an advertisement for a Colonial American Living Room Suite in the daily paper. We find a color TV in the Sunday supplement. Sometimes the Representative appears on our TV, in one dimension, since it is only a two-dimensional set; and he talks about power. Other men appear, talking about Power to the People, the Power Struggle in South Erewhon, the Orderly Transfer of Power, the Power Shortage, and so on. It was a tricky job cutting out the little tiny paper cord and plug for the TV set, but it works fine.

Your Highness:

I am still looking for a Representative Person of Earth, but there seems to have been a power failure somewhere. Please give me some time.

Who Is a True Friend?

Christa C. Porter

Student, Ohio State University

Presented to
a presentational speaking class, Ohio State University,
Columbus, Ohio, spring, 1993

*In this presentation, Christa C. Porter assumed the role
of a teacher of a high-school Sunday school class.*

Good morning, y'all.

Class members: Good morning.

Today, we're going to talk about something you all know a lot about;
I hope we'll get some new ideas on the subject that will stay in your
heads when you leave and get on the church bus. We're going to
talk about friendship. Anybody here have friends?

Class members: Yes.

What is your definition of a true friend? Someone give me a
definition of a true friend.

Class member: Somebody who's loyal and who can be trusted.

OK! Somebody else?

Class member: Somebody you can talk with.

All right. Anyone else?

Class member: Someone to do things with and have fun with.

Used by permission of Christa C. Porter.

OK. Everyone has their own definition of a friend. I'd like to add mine to the list. One of my definitions is that a friend is someone who will respect what I say. Even if my opinions are different from theirs, they'll still respect me and won't call me stupid. A friend is also someone I can call at 3:00 in the morning and say, "I need somebody to talk to," and she'll talk to me. That's what I consider a friend. Even if she has to wake up at 3:00 in the morning, she's willing to talk to me when I need help.

The Bible has some things to say about friends. Proverbs 18:24 says a friend is closer than any brother. Proverbs 27:10: Far better is the neighbor that is nearer than a brother that is far off. And greater love hath no man than this that a man lay down his life for his friend.

OK, you've given me your definitions of a friend, I've given you my definition, and I've given you some of what the Bible says about friends. We've been looking at friendship from our perspective here—of what friends do for us. How about looking at friendship from the other side? How can we be a good friend? Would I wake up at 3:00 in the morning for my friend—to listen to her? If your friend were stranded 20 miles away, would you go pick her up? So, a lot of times, we think about what we want our friends to do, but we never think about what we would do for our friends.

One of the ways in which we can be good friends to others is by being trustworthy, which Regina mentioned in her definition of a friend. Can I keep a secret? Can I be trusted? Trust. That's a common word that is used in the definition of a friend. You've probably all had the experience of having friends talk about you behind your back, they say bad things about you, they tell your business to everyone. The Bible recognizes this potential problem. Proverbs 18:24 says that he that maketh many friends doeth it to his own destruction. A prime example: If you tell your friend something, your friend could have a friend who has a friend who has a friend. And the next thing you know, your business is around the whole school.

Help me out here—you stand up. Now pick out somebody real quick who's your friend. OK, now you pick out somebody who's your friend, and you stand up. One more time—you pick out someone who is your friend. Now, I could tell her about my conversation with a guy from school, she could tell her something, and she could tell him something, and he then tells it to his friend, over here. And by the time it gets back to me, according to the story, I've had a date with this guy, we've had sex, I got pregnant, and I had an abortion—all that from just telling one person one thing. That's what happens when you have a lot of friends, especially the kind who aren't trustworthy.

The whole point of this is the person you can really have trust in is God. You don't have to worry about Him coming down and saying, "Guess what she did last night?" He's going to be there for you regardless, he's going to listen to you, and he's going to give you the best advice. Our friends can be wonderful, but God is the best friend of all.

A Statement for Voices Unheard
A Challenge to the National Book Awards

Adrienne Rich, Audre Lorde, and Alice Walker

Authors

Presented at
the National Book Award ceremony, 1974

At the National Book Award ceremony, Adrienne Rich read the following statement, prepared by herself, Audre Lorde, and Alice Walker—all of whom had been nominated for the poetry award. They agreed that whoever was chosen to receive the award, if any, from among the three, would read the statement.

We, Audre Lorde, Adrienne Rich, and Alice Walker, together accept this award in the name of all the women whose voices have gone and still go unheard in a patriarchal world, and in the name of those who, like us, have been tolerated as token women in this culture, often at great cost and in great pain. We believe that we can enrich ourselves more in supporting and giving to each other than by competing against each other; and that poetry—if it *is* poetry— exists in a realm beyond ranking and comparison. We symbolically join together here in refusing the terms of patriarchal competition and declaring that we will share this prize among us, to be used as best we can for women.

We appreciate the good faith of the judges for this award, but none of us could accept this money for herself, nor could she let go unquestioned the terms on which poets are given or denied honor and livelihood in this world, especially when they are women. We dedicate this occasion to the struggle for self-determination of all women, of every color, identification, or derived class: the poet, the housewife, the lesbian, the mathematician, the mother, the dishwasher, the pregnant teenager, the teacher, the grandmother, the prostitute, the philosopher, the waitress, the women who will understand what we are doing here and those who will not understand yet, the silent women whose voices have been denied us, the articulate women who have given us strength to do our work.

Notes

1. Sherveen Lotfi, paper on speech preparation completed for Communication 505, Ohio State University, June 1993.

2. The notion of an invitation to transformation comes from Sally Miller Gearhart and Sonia Johnson. See, for example: Sally Miller Gearhart, "The Womanization of Rhetoric," *Women's Studies International Quarterly* 2 (1979): 195–201; Sally Miller Gearhart, "Whose Woods These Are," Western Speech Communication Association Convention, Portland, Oregon, Feb. 1980; Sally Gearhart, "Womanpower: Energy Re-Sourcement," *The Politics of Women's Spirituality: Essays on the Rise of Spiritual Power within the Feminist Movement*, ed. Charlene Spretnak (Garden City, NY: Anchor, 1982) 194–206; Sally Miller Gearhart, *The Wanderground: Stories of the Hill Women* (Boston: Alyson, 1984); Sonia Johnson, *Wildfire: Igniting the She/Volution* (Albuquerque: Wildfire, 1989); and Sonia Johnson, *The Ship That Sailed Into the Living Room: Sex and Intimacy Reconsidered* (Estancia, NM: Wildfire, 1991).

3. Lotfi.

4. Gearhart, "The Womanization of Rhetoric" 198.

5. These conditions are derived, in part, from: Sonja K. Foss and Cindy L. Griffin, "Beyond Persuasion: A Proposal for an Invitational Rhetoric," Speech Communication Association Convention, Miami, Florida, Nov. 1993; and Syla Benhabib, *Situating the Self: Gender, Community and Postmodernism in Contemporary Ethics* (New York: Routledge, 1992).

6. This term was coined by Sally Miller Gearhart in "Womanpower."

7. Starhawk, *Truth or Dare: Encounters with Power, Authority, and Mystery* (San Francisco: Harper and Row, 1987) 5.

8. Adrienne Rich, Audre Lorde, and Alice Walker, "A Statement for Voices Unheard: A Challenge to the National Book Awards," *Ms.* 3 (Sept. 1974): 21.

9. These elements are derived largely from Betty Cain, *Beyond Outlining: New Approaches to Rhetorical Form* (Lanham, MD: UP of America, 1992) 34.

10. David Boaz, "The Public School Monopoly: America's Berlin Wall," *Vital Speeches of the Day* 58 (1 June 1992): 507–11.

11. Richard R. Kelley, "Prospering in '92: How to Avoid a Cold When the World is Sneezing," *Vital Speeches of the Day* 58 (1 June 1992): 333–36.

12. The motivated sequence was developed by Alan Monroe. See Douglas Ehninger, Bruce E. Gronbeck, Ray E. McKerrow, and Alan H. Monroe, *Principles and Types of Speech Communication*, 10th ed. (Glenview, IL: Scott, Foresman, 1986) 153.

13. Gearhart, "Whose Woods These Are."

14. Anne Noggle, *Silver Lining: Photographs by Anne Noggle* (Albuquerque: U of New Mexico P, 1983) 29–33.

15. Kenneth Burke, *Permanence and Change: An Anatomy of Purpose* (Indianapolis: Bobbs-Merrill, 1965) 69.

16. Ti-Grace Atkinson, *Amazon Odyssey* (New York: Link, 1974) 191–97.

17. Samuel L. Becker, "Tolerance is Not Enough," *Vital Speeches of the Day* 57 (1 July 1991): 575–76.

18. Garrison Keillor, monologue, "A Prairie Home Companion," 5 Sept. 1987.

19. Jacob Neusner, "Graduates Told: As of Now, Failure Counts," *Tulsa Tribune*, 9 June 1981: C12.

20. Jesse Jackson, "Common Ground and Common Sense," *Vital Speeches of the Day* 54 (15 Aug. 1988): 650.

21. Suzanne Pharr, "The Christian Right: A Threat to Democracy," *Transformation* 7 (Sept./Oct. 1992): 9.

22. Patricia Roberts Harris, "The Law and Moral Issues,"*American Public Discourse: A Multicultural Perspective*, ed. Ronald K. Burke (Lanham, MD: UP of America, 1992) 84.

23. L. Douglas Wilder, "I am a Son of Virginia," *Representative American Speeches, 1989–1990*, ed. Owen Peterson, vol. 62 (New York: H. W. Wilson, 1991) 154.

24. Martin Luther King, Jr., "I Have a Dream," *Contemporary American Public Discourse*, ed. Halford Ross Ryan, 3rd ed. (Prospect Heights, IL: Waveland 1992) 214–17.

25. Walt Bresette, "We Are All Mohawks," *Green Letter* (Winter 1990): 49.

26. Gwen Moffat, quoted in Nina Winter, *Interview with the Muse: Remarkable Women Speak on Creativity and Power* (Berkeley: Moon, 1978) 123.

27. Alan Alda, "Commencement Address at Drew University,"*Contemporary American Speeches: A Sourcebook of Speech Forms and Principles*, ed. Richard L. Johannesen, R. R. Allen, and Wil A. Linkugel, 6th ed. (Dubuque: Kendall/Hunt, 1988) 111.

28. Les Aspin, "Desert One to Desert Storm: Making Ready for Victory," *Vital Speeches of the Day* 57 (15 July 1991): 585.

29. Spiro T. Agnew, "Television News Coverage," *Contemporary American Voices: Significant Speeches in American History, 1945–Present*, ed. James R. Andrews and David Zarefsky (New York: Longman, 1992) 270.

30. John F. Kennedy, "Inaugural Address," *Three Centuries of American Rhetorical Discourse: An Anthology and a Review*, ed. Ronald F. Reid (Prospect Heights, IL: Waveland, 1988) 713.

31. Linda H. Hollies, "A Daughter Survives Incest: A Retrospective Analysis," *Double Stitch: Black Women Write about Mothers and Daughters*, ed. Patricia Bell-Scott, Beverly Guy-Sheftall, Jacqueline Jones Royster, Janet Sims-Wood, Miriam DeCosta-Willis, and Lucie Fultz (Boston: Beacon, 1991) 152.

32. Bresette 50.

33. Russell Means, "For the World to Live, 'Europe' Must Die," *Contemporary American Speeches: A Sourcebook of Speech Forms and Principles*, ed. Richard L. Johannesen, R. R. Allen, and Wil A. Linkugel, 7th ed. (Dubuque: Kendall/Hunt, 1992) 137.

34. Andrei Codrescu, "What Central-European Artists & Writers Can Do for Us, with Remarks on Missouri," *Artlogue* [Missouri Arts Council] 12 (March 1991): 7.

35. Harvey Milk, "The Hope Speech," Randy Shilts, *The Mayor of Castro Street: The Life and Times of Harvey Milk* (New York: St. Martin's, 1982) 360.

36. Chief Weninock, quoted in T. C. McLuhan, ed., *Touch the Earth: A Self-Portrait of Indian Existence* (New York: Touchstone, 1971) 10.

37. Patti P. Gillespie, "1987 Presidential Address: Campus Stories, or The Cat Beyond the Canvas," *Spectra* [Speech Communication Association], Jan. 1988: 3.

38. Ursula K. Le Guin, *Dancing at the Edge of the World: Thoughts on Words, Women, Places* (New York: Grove, 1989) 159.

39. Barbara Brown Zikmund, "What is Our Place?" *And Blessed Is She: Sermons by Women*, ed. David Albert Farmer and Edwina Hunter (San Francisco: Harper and Row, 1990) 233.

40. Janet Hughes, statement presented at the opening of the Missouri Visual Artists' Biennial, University of Missouri, Columbia, 5 Mar. 1993.

41. Ted Koppel, "The Vannatizing of America," *Representative American Speeches 1987–1988*, ed. Owen Peterson, vol. 60 (New York: H. W. Wilson, 1988) 50, 52.
42. Isidore Okpewho, *African Oral Literature: Backgrounds, Character, and Continuity* (Bloomington: Indiana UP, 1992) 53.
43. Diane Stein, *Casting the Circle: A Women's Book of Ritual* (Freedom, CA: Crossing, 1990) 178.
44. Michael L. Hecht, Mary Jane Collier, and Sidney A. Ribeau, *African American Communication: Ethnic Identity and Cultural Interpretation* (Newbury Park, CA: Sage, 1993) 99.
45. Barbara Kingsolver, *The Bean Trees* (New York: Harper Perennial, 1988) 163.
46. Antonia C. Novello, "Alcohol & Tobacco Advertising: Prevention Indeed Works," *Vital Speeches of the Day* 59 (15 May 1993): 457.
47. Shirley Hill Witt, "Past Positives/Present Problems," *American Public Discourse: A Multicultural Perspective*, ed. Ronald K. Burke (Lanham, MD: UP of America, 1992) 10–11.
48. Jesse Jackson, "The Rainbow Coalition," *Contemporary American Public Discourse*, ed. Halford Ross Ryan, 3rd ed. (Prospect Heights, IL: Waveland, 1992) 320.
49. Jesse Jackson, "The Rainbow Coalition" 325.
50. J. D. Salinger, *The Catcher in the Rye* (New York: Bantam, 1951) 58.
51. Umberto Eco, *The Open Work*, trans. Anna Cancogni (Cambridge: Harvard UP, 1989) 166.
52. Peggy Dersch, "Do You Think You Know Me?" *Contemporary American Speeches: A Sourcebook of Speech Forms and Principles*, ed. Richard L. Johannesen, R. R. Allen, and Wil A. Linkugel, 7th ed. (Dubuque: Kendall/Hunt, 1992) 232.
53. Marge Piercy, "Unlearning to Not Speak," Janet Stone and Jane Bachner, *Speaking Up* (New York: McGraw-Hill, 1977) ix.
54. Terry Russell and Renny Russell, *On the Loose* (San Francisco: Sierra Club, 1967) 45.
55. Melodie Lancaster, "The Future We Predict Isn't Inevitable: Reframing Our Success in the Modern World," *Vital Speeches of the Day* 58 (1 Aug. 1992): 636.
56. Kim Woo Choong, "The Korea-America Friendship," *Vital Speeches of the Day*, 58 (1 Oct. 1992): 738.
57. Karen A. Carlton, "Our Lives, One Life," speech presented at commencement ceremonies for the College of Arts and Humanities, Humboldt State University, Arcata, CA, 22 May 1993.
58. George C. Fraser, "Excellence, Education and Perceptions: An African American Crisis," *Vital Speeches of the Day* 58 (15 Nov. 1991): 78.
59. Eleanor Roosevelt, "Address to the Americans for Democratic Action," *Contemporary American Voices: Significant Speeches in American History, 1945–Present*, ed. James R. Andrews and David Zarefsky (New York: Longman, 1992) 26.
60. Dan George, quoted in McLuhan 162.
61. Barbara Jordan, "Democratic Convention Keynote Address," *Contemporary American Public Discourse*, ed. Halford Ross Ryan, 3rd ed. (Prospect Heights, IL: Waveland, 1992) 278.
62. Richard W. Carlson, "When Words Collide: Legal Ethics and the Coming Information Wars," *Vital Speeches of the Day* 54 (15 July 1988): 583.
63. Christine D. Keen, "May You Live in Interesting Times: The Workplace in the '90s," *Vital Speeches of the Day* 58 (15 Nov. 1991): 83–86.
64. Fraser 78–79.
65. Richard L. Weaver II, "Self Motivation: Ten Techniques for Activating or Freeing

the Spirit," *Vital Speeches of the Day* 57 (1 Aug. 1991): 623.

66. Mario Vargas Llosa, "Cherish Liberty: The Loss of Democracy in Peru," *Vital Speeches of the Day* 58 (1 Oct. 1992): 758.